GOD OF COMPASSION

God of
Compassion

Gerard W. Hughes

Hodder & Stoughton

LONDON SYDNEY AUCKLAND

Copyright © 1998 Gerard W. Hughes

First published in Great Britain 1998 by CAFOD,
Romero Close, Stockwell Road, London, SW9 9TY
and Hodder and Stoughton Ltd

British Library Cataloguing in Publication Data
A record for this book is available from the British Library

ISBN 0 340 69487 4

Typeset by Avon Dataset Ltd, Bidford-on-Avon, Warks

Printed and bound in Great Britain by
Mackays of Chatham plc, Chatham, Kent

Hodder and Stoughton
A division of Hodder Headline PLC
338 Euston Road
London NW1 3BH

Contents

Acknowledgments

To Brendan Walsh of CAFOD, who invited me to write this book, for his constant encouragement and for organising a visit to São Paulo. To Brian Davies of CAFOD, Sjef Donders and Ralph Woodhall for their helpful comments. To Janet Morley of Christian Aid, whose original idea was the inspiration for this book. To Teresa de Bertodano for her patient and meticulous editing. To Julie Ambrose of Hodder & Stoughton for her management of the editorial process.

Preface

This book was originally entitled 'The Heart of the Matter', because the fact that God has made a Covenant with the whole of creation is at the heart of all matters.

The book has an introduction, which includes a brief exploration of the meaning of God's Covenant. The introduction also suggests some methods of prayer with which the reader can experiment, and methods of reflection which can be undertaken individually or in groups.

The second part of the book consists of reflections on fifty Bible texts, which illustrate the meaning of God's Covenant with us and its implications for every aspect of our lives as individuals, as Church, as nation, and in our international relationships. Each text and commentary is followed by a short prayer and an 'exercise'. The exercises are offered as a method of deepening our understanding of God's Covenant as it relates to the details of our lives, our feelings and thoughts, and our actions and reactions.

There is an ancient Rabbinic saying, 'Do, and you will understand.' It is only by engaging in some way in the promotion of justice and peace that we can begin to appreciate the significance of God's Cosmic Covenant for every aspect of our lives. There are many different ways of doing this. A useful guiding principle is 'Think globally, act locally.'

To encourage and assist the reader in choosing some practical involvement, there are two Appendices at the end of the book. The first appendix is a practical guide for setting up a 'New Covenant with the Poor', a proposal for parishes in celebration of the Third Millennium.

The second appendix contains an alphabetical list of some of the many voluntary organisations which engage in some form of reconciliation work, and promote justice and peace.

Before completing this book I paid a brief visit to Brazil, where I met people who are supported by CAFOD in their work among the homeless of São Paulo, Brazil's largest city. The city itself numbers ten million, of whom two million live in 'favellas'; homemade houses of plywood, cardboard and plastic covering. Another five million live in slums; houses built of more durable material. I was familiar with the word favella, but I had never before met the children, women and men who live in these dwellings. Favellas are the dwellings of the destitute, some driven from their land by drought, the majority by wealthy landowners, just as the Scots were driven off their land in the Highland clearances of the last century. In Brazil the clearances are on a more massive scale and the landless pour into São Paulo in search of work. Finding neither jobs nor shelter, they search for waste ground, often under viaducts to protect them from the rain, where they build themselves shacks from scavenged plywood and plastic sheets. Here they live, unsupported by any state aid, making a living by scavenging among the rubbish dumps and scrap heaps until death releases them. Yet Brazil is one of the world's wealthiest countries, covering an area larger than the USA.

Father Paddy McGhee, a Lancashire man of many gifts, who has been working in São Paulo for years and is currently teaching computer skills to favella children, told me that, in spite of years of study, he had never understood the Bible until he met these biblical people in Brazil. Another priest working in São Paulo, David Regan, told me that he, like many Westerners, used to dislike the vengeance passages of the Old Testament prophets and of the Psalms, finding them barbaric and better omitted in polite company. Having lived among the destitute, he now understands these passages very clearly.

PREFACE

It is out of the experience of poverty in South and Central American countries, and out of people's reflection on it in the light of the Bible, that Liberation Theology was born. Liberation Theology is not an invention of the twentieth century, but is the recovery of a biblical reality to which scripture scholars and theologians paid scant attention until, in the 1960s, some of them began to share their lives with the poor, and saw the ravages of poverty on a scale far greater than anything experienced by the Old Testament prophets. Liberation Theology is rooted in the experience of the Latin-American poor, especially that of the base ecclesiastical communities. These are communities of peasants and workers who, reading the Word of God within their own context of oppression and exploitation, discover the Bible to be a source of empowerment and liberation. With its message of the goodness of creation and of God's universal love for humankind, expressed most clearly in the life, suffering, death and Resurrection of Jesus, the Bible stands in judgment over the dehumanising conditions under which the poor live, and it empowers them to work for that justice which is God's will. For the oppressed, God's love takes the form of liberation: for the oppressors, it takes the form of a call to conversion and disempowerment. 'He has pulled down princes from their thrones and raised high the lowly' (Luke 1:52).

The problems of hunger and homelessness, and the widening gap between rich and poor, are not unique to Brazil; they are even worse in some other countries, and they afflict us, too, in Western Europe. In every country there is hope that a change of government will remedy the situation, but the slow war against poverty rolls on relentlessly. A diminishing number of people grow wealthier, while an increasing number are deprived of the bare necessities of life. Why?

One answer, frequently given, is that the problem is caused by our global economy, as though this is a destructive force of nature over which we have no control. But the global economy is something freely chosen by those in power. It is not of divine necessity that in today's world 385 of the wealthiest individuals have more wealth at their disposal than 2.2 billion others, almost half the world's population. Nor is it a natural necessity that we should spend sums of money annually on weapons of death which, if applied to the hungry and homeless of the world, could provide them with adequate food, water, shelter and basic health care. There is nothing immutable about the national debts which burden Third World countries and which cause governments and landlords to drive people from their land and living. Land, which provided subsistence crops for local people, is now used for growing luxury crops for sale to wealthy nations, thus enabling governments to pay the interest charges on their national debt. In Brazil, for example, thousands have been driven off their land, where crops are now grown to provide cattle feed for European countries. Besides being cruel, inhuman and unjust, the imposition of these crushing interest charges halts development in Third World countries, and will eventually impoverish the wealthy countries as well.

This makes depressing reading, and those of us who are reasonably secure, a security ensured by these unjust structures, might prefer not to dwell on these problems, but the problems are not confined to the victims of material poverty. The affluent, who wish to remain unaware of the problem, are also victims, because they are deprived of their humanity, the greatest deprivation of all. Living in their wealthy ghettoes, surrounded by security systems, they are fearful, anxious and isolated, not only from the poor, but also from themselves.

In São Paulo, another priest, Fr Pat Clarke, a poet, writer and thinker, who works full-time in the favellas, told me of one shack he visited, where he found a large picture of the Sacred Heart. 'Where did you find this?' he asked the family. 'We found it in the rubbish dump, and he looked so sad and lonely that we took him in, so that he will always have a home, wherever we are.' What a profound insight into the nature of God, who is Love!

In the Hebrew Bible, the poor are called the 'Anawim', which means, 'The bent-over ones'. It is from the Anawim that salvation will come. To ignore them is to ignore God, no matter how many hymns we sing, or religious services we attend.

Introduction

The Bible is the common inheritance of all Christians. In every country where it has taken root, stories and images of the Bible, its wisdom and teachings, have affected every aspect of life: music, drama, literature and art, as well as legal, political, social and economic structures. At this point some readers may be thinking, 'And a fine mess it has made, causing divisions among peoples, murderous conflicts, oppression of peoples, exploitation of natural resources, all in the name of God and country.'

At one time the Bible was known as the Open Book, open to all people. Today, in Britain at least, the Bible is no longer the Open Book; it is closed for most people. But the era of the closed book has not been marked by any lessening of violence and destruction. G.K. Chesterton wrote, 'It is not that Christianity has been tried and found wanting: it has not been tried.'

In this book we are going to reflect on Chesterton's statement by focusing on the meaning of Covenant. Covenant, literally, means 'a coming together', 'a meeting'. The Hebrew prophets speak of the coming together of God and Israel as a marriage. The Bible describes Israel's dawning awareness that the One God of all creation has called her into an everlasting Covenant. 'I will be your God, and you shall be my people.' Israel is called to mirror the holiness of God in every detail of her life, in her relationships within the nation, but also with the stranger. The different books of the Bible explore the nature, meaning and implications of this Covenant. The fifty texts which follow this introduction continue the exploration in our own lives today.

The Covenant was revealed to the Hebrew people, and they are chosen to become a 'Light to the Nations'. God's marriage is not just to the Hebrew people, but through Israel to all human beings and, as we shall see in the texts which follow, not only to all human beings, but to all creation – plants and animals, oceans and rivers. St Paul writes of Christ:

> He is the image of the unseen God and the first-born of all creation, for in him were created all things in heaven and on earth: everything visible and everything invisible, Thrones, Dominations, Sovereignties, Powers – all things were created through him and for him. Before anything was created, he existed, and he holds all things in unity. Now the Church is his body, he is its head.
>
> (Colossians 1: 15–18)

God's Covenant not only affects all human beings and all creation; it affects every aspect of life, not only our external behaviour, but also the way we think, how we see the world, and, therefore, the way in which we react to it.

One of the reasons for Christianity's failure is that we have domesticated God, making religion a private matter between the individual and God; or a national matter, loyalty to one's nation becoming synonymous with loyalty to God, so that we say of those who have died in our wars that they died *Pro Deo et Patria*, 'for God and country'. In this way, religion can become a powerful and deadly source of conflict between individuals and between nations. The Jewish mystic, Martin Buber, wrote, 'Nothing so masks the face of God as religion'!

In São Paulo, I saw much evidence of the popularity of American evangelism, which is winning over many of the poor from the Catholic Church which used to number 89 per cent of the population of Brazil. Among middle-class Catholics, the Charismatic movement is becoming increasingly popular. Many of the Evangelical and Pentecostal churches of the USA, preach a 'Gospel of Prosperity' – 'Invest in God and he will give you good returns, even a hundred-fold.' These churches attract the poor with their lively services of praise and thanksgiving, their occasional handouts and the opportunity for quick promotion to preacher status for regular attenders. There is the promise of prosperity in this world, and salvation in the next for those who turn to Jesus, provided they pay tithes of their meagre earnings in support of their church. The Charismatic movement, with its emphasis on praise and thanksgiving, pleases the middle classes because it enables participants to see their prosperity as a mark of God's favour, while relieving them of any nagging compassion for the sufferings of their destitute brothers and sisters. While both the American Evangelicals and the Catholic Charismatics certainly help individuals, too few of them appear to question the political, social and economic structures which are oppressing the poor majority. Such an attitude, of course, makes them popular with their governments, with the multinationals, and with wealthy landowners.

The basic Christian communities, which were so lively and effective in renewing the Church in Latin America in the 1960s, '70s and '80s, are now in decline in Brazil. In the 1960s and the 1970s they had a clear enemy, the military dictatorship. Under the democratic government which followed, the poor still suffer even worse deprivation. Their great church leaders, including Archbishop Helder Camara of Recife, Cardinal Arns of São Paulo and Archbishop Lohrscheider, are now growing old and a number of recent episcopal appointments by Rome reflect the Vatican's continuing unease with Liberation Theology, despite the fact that recent Papal documents acknowledge the Liberation Theology of the Bible.

Should the Church be concerned with political, social and economic structures? The readings which follow will, I hope, make it clear that the promotion of justice is not an optional extra for Christians of leftish tendencies, but is the essence of

Christian faith. Justice is integral to faith because God, who has made a Covenant with us, is a God of compassion for all creation:

> Yes, you love everything that exists and nothing that you have made disgusts you, since, if you had hated something, you would not have made it. And how could a thing subsist, had you not willed it . . . No, you spare all things, since all is yours, Lord, lover of life, for your imperishable spirit is in everything.
>
> (Wisdom 11:24–12:1)

As compassion is the quality which characterises God in Scripture, compassion must be the distinctive quality of the people of the Covenant. In Luke's account of the Sermon on the Mount Jesus says, 'Be compassionate, as your Heavenly Father is compassionate.' 'Be holy,' God tells Israel, 'as I the Lord your God am holy.' Holiness is the essence of the Covenant. To be holy is to be compassionate towards all creation. Holiness without compassion is a contradiction in terms.

The fact that we are aware that holiness requires us to mirror in our lives the compassion of God for all creation does not necessarily make us any more compassionate towards our brothers and sisters. We are very complex creatures, with layer upon layer of consciousness, as well as a subconscious. Each layer affects our perception of the world and the way we react to it. Knowledge of the Bible and of theology can lodge in our minds at a superficial level and can be useful in satisfying examiners. Such knowledge does not necessarily make us more compassionate. That is why we need to pray the Bible, not merely to study it. Prayer and study are two different activities. Study can remain on the surface of our minds and may have no effect on our behaviour: prayer can reach the deepest levels of our souls and bring about a change of mind and heart.

The texts and commentaries which follow are designed for prayer and reflection, not for study. If you pray the passages, you may not do very well in a Scripture exam, but you will gain something much more precious, for it is in prayer that we allow God to be the God of Compassion to us and through us.

Guidelines on Prayer

These are some very simple guidelines on prayer which may help you to pray the passages which follow.

1   In prayer, 'heart speaks to Heart': however you pray, let it be simple and from the heart, as friend talks to friend. In general, follow the excellent advice of Dom John Chapman, 'Pray as you can, not as you can't', and follow your own inner promptings.

2   If you feel, 'But I *can't* pray', that is a sign of progress! You have discovered the truth, for there is a sense in which none of us can pray: God prays within us. All we can do in prayer is 'be still', as the Psalmist says, and let God pray in us. Prayer is like the verse at the beginning of the Bible, 'Now the earth was a formless void, and the spirit of God hovered over the chaos' (Genesis 1:2). We are the chaos! In prayer, let the Spirit of God hover over you, producing light and order out of your darkness and chaos.

3   Find as quiet a place as you can, and decide before you begin how long you are going to give to prayer. However restless you may feel, give that amount of time. There are many layers of consciousness within us. Before reaching a deeper layer, we often experience inner emptiness and feel that nothing is happening. If we abandon prayer every time it ceases to be 'interesting', we fail to reach the deeper layers of consciousness, where change occurs. You may

lengthen the time of prayer, if you want, but do not shorten it.

4   Read over one of the Scripture passages which follow. If you have a Bible, you may want to read the full passage for which references are given: if not, content yourself with the one or two verses given for each day. Read the verses over slowly, and also the commentary which follows. Do not be in a hurry. If you find a particular verse helps you to pray, then stay with it for as long as you can, for months if you wish. The same applies to the exercises which follow each commentary. If you find one particular exercise helpful, then keep practising it for as long as it holds your interest.

5   Having read over the passage as many times as you want, pause. Notice if any word, phrase or image has struck you in any way. If so, focus on that word or phrase, hear God speaking it to you now, and have a conversation with God. Don't be afraid to complain, grumble, object: God is big enough to take our tantrums. If you do not make time to pray during the day, then at least recall in odd moments the word or phrase which struck you.

6   Most of us, when we begin to pray, are afflicted with 'distractions'. Our minds dart off in directions which apparently have nothing to do with the text we are praying. When you become aware of the distraction, present it to God in prayer. It may be something you need to pray about, and it may become the substance of your prayer. If the distraction is leading you away from praying simply to God in your heart, then let it go, and return to the Bible text.

7   If you are content just to repeat a word, or phrase, then do so. Ideally, all our prayer should eventually lead to silence, like the wonderful description of prayer, 'He looks at me, and I look at Him.'

On Using This Book With Groups

Jesus said, 'Where two or more are gathered, I am there in the midst of them.' However, when two or more are gathered, even for Bible study or sharing, all hell can break loose! So here are some guidelines for using this book with others:

1 Sharing with others will only be of value if those taking part have first spent time praying the Bible passages on their own. This can be done either before the meeting, or you can reserve the first 15–20 minutes of the meeting itself for private prayer in silence, all praying the same passage. You should agree beforehand that anything shared within the group is shared in confidence, otherwise the quality of sharing is likely to remain superficial.

2 Agree on a set time for starting and finishing the meeting, and keep to it. If you are going to offer hospitality, agree beforehand that it should be simple, so that the host is not burdened.

3 These groups are for listening and sharing, NOT FOR DISCUSSION. This is vital. If you follow this guideline, you will discover its benefits: if you do not, the group will soon break up.

4 Take turns to chair the meeting. The chair has two functions: first, to ensure that everyone who wants to speak has a chance to do so, and second, to stop anyone who begins to theorise or argue. The rest of the group should be encouraged to sup-

port the chairperson in both these tasks. Theoretical discussion and argument can kill a group very rapidly.

5   What do you share with one another? In so far as you are willing, you share your own experience of trying to pray the Bible passage. For example, what was your felt reaction during and after your prayer? Did you feel at peace or troubled, happy or sad, hopeful or guilty? Did any word, phrase, image or idea strike you? In so far as you are willing to make it known, tell the group why you felt as you did, and why a particular word or phrase struck you in this way? There is no need to analyse what you have experienced, just express it, and in expressing it you will begin to understand more clearly your own experience and its connection with other aspects of your life.

6   As each person speaks in turn, the others listen without any interruption, comment or questioning. It is good to have a short pause after each one has spoken, as a mark of respect for the speaker and to allow what has been shared to sink in.

7   When all who wish to speak have done so, have another pause, to reflect privately on what has been said. It may be that something someone has shared has helped you to come into closer touch with your own experience, and you may want to speak about that. Always avoid theoretical discussion or argument during the sharing.

8   It is good to end the meeting with a few moments of silent prayer, praying for one another and for the needs of the world.

This method of sharing may seem to you to be a very unsatisfactory way of solving the world's problems. Give it a try! Remember the rabbinic saying, 'Do and you will understand.' Among other things, this method of sharing helps us to know that we cannot change the world simply by discussing its problems. Through the discipline of just listening in silence to other people's experiences, we become aware of our own tendency to categorise, judge and moralise, and of our own desire to sort out the problems of the rest of the group. Thus we discover in ourselves the same tendency to control and dominate others which creates a world where billions suffer at the hands of a few. We may also come to realise that ultimately the only thing any of us can change is ourselves, and that the only thing we can change in ourselves is our way of perceiving reality. When we perceive differently, we begin to act differently, which produces reactions in other people, and thus change occurs. By listening to one another without discussion, argument, or any attempt to correct one another, our perceptions can begin to change.

When you read this book, remember the poor and destitute who are mentioned in it, and the people who work with them. In St Augustine's words, 'God is closer to me than I am to myself', but God is also the God of the whole cosmos. Your prayers from your heart have reverberations throughout creation and can bring life and peace to people you have never known, and will probably never meet in this life. 'God's power working in us can do infinitely more than we can think or imagine' (Ephesians 3:20).

Texts and Commentaries

Genesis 1:1–25

Now the earth was a formless void, there was darkness
over the deep, and God's spirit hovered over the water.

(1:2)

The Pentateuch, the name given to the first five books of the
Bible, of which Genesis is the first, contains the basic 'Torah' or
law of Israel. The word 'Pentateuch' comes from the Greek,
meaning 'five-fold scroll', and was completed in the fifth century
before Christ. It is a collection of ancient memories reaching
back several thousand years and drawing on at least four different
traditions.

The Hebrew Scripture in its entirety is a faith autobiography
of Israel, in which she reflects on her history in the light of the
message revealed to her through the centuries by the prophets
and patriarchs – that God had entered into a Covenant with this
tiny nation of refugees, this wandering, homeless people. God
had called them to become 'a light to the nations'. It is very
significant that this history should begin, not with the call of
Abram and Sarai, but with the creation of the whole world. This
sets the whole Covenant story in context, for God is the God of
all creation and his Covenant is cosmic. In these readings, we are
going to reflect on our own history in the light of that same
message. We read the Bible, not primarily to learn about Jewish
history, but in order to understand our own, for the God of Israel
is the God who now holds us in being.

GOD OF COMPASSION

Even when Israel eventually became a nation and reached its peak of power and prosperity under King David a thousand years before Christ, she was surrounded by more powerful and more technically advanced peoples, who held a variety of theories about the meaning of life, but who all perceived human beings as the puppets of warring gods and goddesses. The object of life was to appease the warring deities by performing the appropriate religious rites. Israel's distinctiveness was her unique understanding of God: there is only One God, who is good and loving, and all that God has made is good. This God is continuously at work in history to save the human race, even when it fails Him.

Today's verse is telling us that in all the mess, confusion, tears and tragedy of life today, the Spirit of God is still hovering over the chaos, bringing light out of the darkness, order out of chaos, hope out of hopelessness, life out of death.

In praying this verse, repeat it to yourself several times. Allow the Spirit to hover over your fears, anxieties, frustrations and failures, and talk with God as a friend speaks to a friend. If you have difficulty with the idea of God, are not sure whether God exists, or whether you really believe, then speak with your own heart, for that is your doorway to God's presence. Do you long for light in your darkness, peace amid conflict and anxiety? God is not an object outside you, but is closer to you than you are to yourself. God accepts and welcomes you, and longs for your peace, however chaotic you may feel yourself to be.

PRAYER

Spirit of God, hover over my chaos and over the pain and tears of the world. Bring light to my darkness, order to my disorder, life to my deadness, so that I may become a channel of your goodness.

EXERCISE

Recall any occasion in your life when you have found life and order emerging from chaos.

Genesis 1:26–31

> God created humankind in the image of himself,
> in the image of God he created them,
> male and female he created them. (1:27)

In the creation accounts of Middle-Eastern nations surrounding Israel, women were considered inferior, ranking as the chattels of men, along with sheep and oxen! The creation account of Israel differs, not only in stating that there is only One God, but also in declaring that all women, as well as all men, are made in the image of God. And this creation account is also unique in affirming that everything God has created is good.

This teaching may be very familiar to us, but in the light of Christianity's history, it is a lesson we have still to learn.

We are made in the image of God. God, in Christian understanding, is a God of Three Persons: Father, Son and Holy Spirit. This mystery of the Trinity leaves most of us baffled, yet if we are made in the image of God, it must be saying something about ourselves and who we are.

Although God is Three Persons, these Three Persons, nevertheless, relate to one another so totally that there is no inequality between them: their life is a complete sharing, a total communion.

We, on the other hand, tend to think of ourselves primarily as individuals who then relate to others. The doctrine of the Trinity suggests that our perception is the wrong way round, and that we only exist insofar as we relate. Although we may often wish God had not ordained it thus, the reality is that any movement, whether religious or secular, which ignores the plight of the destitute, is moving in opposition to God.

What are the ultimate constituents of matter? The Greeks reckoned that there must be some basic building blocks, so they called them atoms, which means 'that which cannot be divided'. Some modern nuclear physicists have conjectured that there are no ultimate constituents of matter, but that in every particle is contained every other particle, for everything that exists, exists in relation to everything else. We are interdependent and interconnected with one another in ways we are only beginning to understand.

'Love the Lord, Your God, with all your heart and soul and mind and strength, and your neighbour as yourself.' Why? Because your neighbour *is* yourself, and it is only possible to find God by the way we relate to one another. 'As you did to one of these least,' Jesus says in his account of the Final Judgment in Matthew 25, 'you were doing to me.'

PRAYER
God, dispel the darkness of our minds, and lead us gently to the truth of your presence, and of our own, in all the people we encounter, so that we can see our lives as a gift given that others may live, especially the hungry and destitute.

EXERCISE
Draw up two columns on a piece of paper, one headed 'Events which enliven me', the other 'Events which deaden me'. Look through each list carefully. In each list, where was the focus of your attention – on yourself, or on other people and other things?

Genesis 3:1–24

'Where are you?' asked Yahweh God. (3:9)

Adam and Eve, having eaten the apple, become aware of their nakedness and hide from God, so God asks 'Where are you?'

The ancient creation myths, which were current in the Middle East when the book of Genesis was being written, were attempts to answer the question, 'What is the origin of evil?' The myths, as we saw in the first of these passages, located the origin of evil outside human beings, and in warring gods and goddesses. The Hebrew answer was that evil is not outside us, for all creation is good, but rather that it lies within the human mind and heart. We may consider this an inadequate answer, but before dismissing it, we need to ask whether or not it contains some measure of truth.

The tendency to project the blame for our own misfortunes onto others is in all of us. We all like to think ourselves innocent victims of the malice, or stupidity of others, so we blame our genetic make-up, parental upbringing, teachers, employers, the current government, or Church authorities. While this may provide temporary relief, it changes nothing, for it fails to touch the root of the problem, which lies in our own minds and hearts.

In Hebrew, our word 'Adam' means 'a human being'. The first chapters of the book of Genesis describe the nature and effect of human sin in Hebrew fashion by clothing the truth in story form, but the message of the story applies to all people at all times.

The effect of sin on Adam and Eve is three-fold: they

experience division within themselves and so become ashamed of their nakedness; they become divided from one another, Adam blaming Eve; and both become divided from God, so they hide.

All of us, sooner or later, become aware of our 'shadow-self', as the analytical psychologist Carl Jung described it. We do not like this and try to disown the shadow by projecting it onto others. Consequently, Adam starts blaming Eve. We have to find an 'enemy' in order to justify ourselves. We do this individually, nationally and internationally. Wealthy countries, having exploited the Third World, continue to oppress and exploit, blaming the threat of Communism as 'the enemy' and making this threat a justification for continued oppression. In our own country, the blame for inner-city poverty and unemployment has been laid upon its victims: they are called layabouts, work-shy, scroungers on the state. If we lose one enemy, e.g. Soviet Russia, we must quickly find another, lest we are forced to look at the evil within ourselves.

Sin is dividedness. Adam's son, Cain, kills his brother Abel. As the divisions continue, multiply and intensify, each section becomes more fearful of the other and feels the need to defend itself. Every year, world powers spend more money on weapons of destruction than on the prevention of disease or food and shelter for the homeless, with the result that we now possess enough nuclear weaponry to destroy all human life on earth.

PRAYER

God, lead me and lead our nation out of the prison of our own self-protection, which threatens the lives of millions of people. Heal us of the blindness which prevents us from seeing that oppression of others is oppression of ourselves.

EXERCISE

Hear God calling you by name and asking 'Where are you?' Hiding behind lies, behind status, behind self-importance? God is in truth, and the truth sets us free. All we have to do is acknowledge that we are hiding. God will gently lead us out to truth, and into reconciliation with ourselves and with others.

Genesis 6:1–9:29

> For my part I mean to bring a flood – everything on earth
> will perish. But I will establish my Covenant with you.
>
> (6:17–18)

The story of the Flood appears in many ancient myths, but the
Hebrew account contains themes which keep recurring
throughout the Bible, and which we can recognise in our lives
today.

One theme is the close link between nature and the human
heart. We are much more closely linked with one another and
with all creation than we realise. The story of the Flood is an
assertion that human life and the whole earth are affected by
human wickedness. However, just as human wickedness can
destroy, so human goodness can save humankind and nature from
destruction, as was the case with Noah.

Another theme within the Hebrew account of the Flood is the
involvement of God. God tells Noah that the rainbow which
appears after the Flood is 'the sign of the Covenant I have
established between myself and every living thing that is found
on the earth' (9:17).

The physical sciences today are aware of the mysterious inter-
relationship of every particle in the universe, a link graphically
expressed in the phrase, 'When a baby throws its rattle out of the
cradle, the planets rock!'

The twelfth-century Rhineland mystic, Hildegard of Bingen,

was aware, not only of the close physical connection between all things, but also of the close spiritual connection. We affect one another and all nature by the disposition of our hearts. In one of her poems, Hildegard writes:

> Now in the people
> that were meant to green,
> there is no more life of any kind.
> There is only shrivelled barrenness –
> Thunderstorms menace.
> The air belches out
> the filthy uncleanness of the peoples.

When afflicted by a sense of our total powerlessness to effect any change in ourselves or in the world, it is worth asking 'Who do I think I am?' St Paul tells us that 'God working in us can do infinitely more than we can ask or imagine' (Ephesians 3:20). Prayer is about letting God be God to us and through us. Present your feelings of helplessness to God and pray that his Spirit may be released in you for the benefit of us all, especially those who are hungry, homeless and destitute.

PRAYER

God, make me more aware of my interconnectedness and dependence on all creation, and of my total dependence on you. Cleanse my heart of all its meanness and petty-mindedness, and fill it with your compassion for all creation.

EXERCISE

Stare at the palm of your hand and reflect on your interconnectedness! It can take you back to the origin of the species, to all those who nurtured you, to those who toiled to grow the food which has nourished you, to the earth which mothers the plants and animals which sustain you, to the sun without which nothing could grow! 'No man is an island.'

Genesis 11:1–9

'Come,' they said 'let us build ourselves a town and a
tower with its top reaching to heaven.' (11:4)

According to the story of the Tower of Babel, all human beings
spoke the same language until they decided to build a tower 'with
its top reaching to heaven. Let us make a name for ourselves, so
that we may not be scattered about the whole earth.' This plan
displeases God, who confuses their language so that they can no
longer understand one another. From Babel 'Yahweh scattered
them over the whole earth.'

What is the meaning of the story? The people of Babel
represent human attempts to take over from God and to control
the world in our own fashion, creating our own security: 'Let us
make a name for ourselves, so that we may not be scattered over
the whole earth.' Their plan is frustrated. Divided from God, they
become divided among themselves and can no longer understand
one another. This sentence is a succinct summary of world history
and of the lives of each one of us!

'Let us make a name for ourselves' is an apparently laudable
ambition, but by so doing we identify ourselves by the ways in
which we differ from others. Donald Nicholl, historian and
religious writer, once arrived in my room straight from a meeting.
'It was one of those dreadful meetings,' he said, 'in which we all
had to introduce ourselves at the beginning. Each person present
defined themselves by their profession: "I am a teacher, a doctor,

24

a banker, etc." When it came to my turn, all that I wanted to say was "My name is Donald: I am a unique manifestation of God!" '

If we identify ourselves by our differences, we cling to those differences with all the power of our instinct for self-preservation, the strongest of all our instincts. In our struggle to be different, we oppress, exploit and even eliminate any who threaten what we deem to be our very existence. This process leads to the disintegration of society and to the reign of individualism. Violence increases, mutual trust perishes, and we become separated from one another, locked into the prison of our own self-interest.

As we separate ourselves from others and destroy, or ignore their wellbeing in our pursuit of our individual interest, we become separated from our very self, for we can only find that self insofar as we live in unity, recognising the other, whoever the other may be, as we recognise ourselves. That is why the greatest of all the commandments is 'To love the Lord, our God, with all our heart and soul, mind and strength, and to love our neighbour as we love ourselves'.

PRAYER
God, free me from my conditioning which leads me to compete rather than to co-operate, to destroy rather than to build up.

EXERCISE
'In our struggle to be different, we oppress, exploit, and try to eliminate any who threaten what we deem to be our very existence.' Reflect on the damage we can do to ourselves and to others when we identify ourselves by our differences.

Genesis 15:1–21

> When the sun had set and darkness had fallen, there
> appeared a smoking furnace and a firebrand that went
> between the halves. That day Yahweh made a Covenant
> with Abram. (15:17–18)

In ancient times, nomadic peoples used to make covenants with
each other for their mutual profit and protection. The covenant
was ratified in a solemn ceremony. An animal was taken, killed,
and its dismembered parts laid upon the ground. The contracting
parties then walked between the dismembered parts, praying that
they should suffer the same fate as the dismembered animal if
they were to break the covenant.

In this text, God has called Abram out of his own land to
inherit a new country. Abram asks, 'How am I to know that I
shall inherit it?' God tells Abram to take a goat and a ram, and to
cut them in half. When darkness falls, Abram sees a firebrand
passing between the halves, sign of God entering into a Covenant
with him and with his descendants.

In the Bible, there is a developing understanding of who God
is. 'Yahweh Sabaoth' denotes a military God, 'Lord God of hosts',
a God who will slay the enemies of God's chosen people, allowing
them to slay and appropriate land in good conscience from
whatever people they consider to be their own enemies, and
therefore enemies of God. Christianity has frequently failed to
advance beyond this notion of God. The Dutch Reformed Church

in South Africa once claimed that Apartheid was of divine ordinance. To deny this was to be labelled a heretic!

The God revealed in later books of the Bible, and in Jesus, is a very different God, a God who has compassion on the whole of creation, who allows the rain to fall on the just and the unjust alike, who identifies with every human being, and whom we meet in every human encounter. 'As you do to one of these least, you are doing to me.' To be chosen by God is to be called to let God be the God of compassion to us and through us.

Christians, both individually and corporately, can still be tempted to think of 'Chosen People' as meaning 'chosen to be superior to', 'chosen to have power over'. The Covenant to which we are called is not a covenant of control, or of domination, but a covenant of love, of self-giving that others may live.

PRAYER
Speak to Christ on the cross and hear God say, 'This is the New Covenant in my blood. This is what I think you are worth.' What do you want to say in reply?

EXERCISE
Each Eucharist that we celebrate is a sign of the Covenant God is making with us and with all creation. In the light of this truth, how would you like the Eucharist to be celebrated?

Exodus 14:15–31

That day, Yahweh rescued Israel from the Egyptians.

(14:30)

The Bible can be described as the faith history of Israel. By reflecting on her own history, Israel becomes more aware of who God is, not only for Israel, but for all peoples.

A key event in Israel's history was its liberation from slavery in Egypt, when they were led through the desert wilderness and into the Promised Land. Each year Jews remember this 'passing over' from slavery to freedom in the 'Passover', in order to remind themselves that the God who then set them free from slavery is the God of the present, a liberating God, continuously leading us from slavery into freedom. Christians see the fulfilment of this Passover in the life, death and Resurrection of Jesus, and we celebrate this deliverance in every Eucharist, but especially at Easter. The celebration is to remind us of a continuous reality at work in all peoples, at all times, because God is constantly leading us out of our slavery, whatever form it may take, through a wilderness and into a Promised Land.

I once worked with a group of men and women, demoralised by years of unemployment and without hope of re-employment. One evening, after reading the Exodus account of the Passover, they sat round in small groups pretending to be Israelites in the desert, with a candle in the midst of each small group. They could identify with the Israelites grumbling against Moses for removing them from the fleshpots of Egypt with its abundance of garlic and cucumbers, and leading them into this hopeless wilderness, for they, too, remembered their years of employment when they could occasionally go to the pub of an evening and even take the family on holiday, whereas now they were trapped in poverty without hope for the future. The eventual effect of this exercise was amazing: it did not produce jobs, but it did bring them hope in their present wilderness.

This text sustains and encourages millions of poor and oppressed people today. Among the destitute in São Paulo, living in favellas, I was struck by the resilience of the people I met. Their living conditions were appalling, their little shacks leaky and cold. Some whom I met were suffering from AIDS, women infected by their husbands, some of whom had then left them with children who were sometimes also AIDS-infected. Yet these women struggle on, sustained by faith in a God who liberates.

One of the women I met in Brazil was Gabriela, an Irish nurse, who has been working in São Paulo for over twenty years. Currently she is working with AIDS victims, creating networks so that the victims can meet and support one another, building clinics to provide basic health care, and helping them to see their suffering as a sharing in Jesus's suffering and death for the salvation of all peoples. Her work is supported by CAFOD, and her Centre is called 'Esparanza', which means 'hope'. God, the liberator, invites and needs our co-operation, which can take many different forms – living with the oppressed, as Gabriela does, supporting her project financially and praying for both the oppressed and their oppressors.

PRAYER

God, who brought Israel out of slavery and into freedom, set us free from the slavery of the conditioning imposed on us, and of the conditioning we have imposed on ourselves. Strengthen us so that we may bring that freedom to others.

EXERCISE

Imagine you are one of the Israelites in the wilderness. They pined for the leeks, garlic and cucumbers which they used to enjoy while in slavery, and they grumbled at their deliverance. Share your own grumbles with them. Then ask God, 'Lord, show me your attractiveness. Fill me with such a longing for you and for your goodness that nothing can ever draw me back into slavery.'

Isaiah 54:4–14

Do not be afraid, you will not be put to shame . . . for
you will forget the shame of your youth . . . For now your
creator will be your husband . . . For the mountains may
depart, the hills be shaken, but my love for you will
never leave you and my covenant of peace with you will
never be shaken, says Yahweh who takes pity on you.

(54:4, 5, 10)

These words of the prophet Isaiah are addressed to the Israelites
in exile in Babylon. Their situation seemed hopeless; their own
city of Jerusalem was a wilderness. The God who then encouraged
them in their hopelessness with such tenderness and compassion
is the God who says to you now, 'For the mountains may depart,
the hills be shaken, but my love for you will never leave you.'

If the Bible is to be an open book for us, its message has to
reach beyond the surface of our minds into the core of our being,
for it is there that change occurs. To reach that core, be still for a
few minutes. Reflect on the mystery, not of God, but of yourself.
Your body consists of billions of cells, each one unique to you,
and each one of such complexity that no scientist would claim to
understand it completely. Each cell contains within it the whole
design of your body. And this mysterious body is linked with
everyone and with everything else in the universe. Out of this
mystery that is yourself, hear today's text being spoken to you.
You are loved and cherished, and that love will never leave you.

You have not earned this love: you do not have to earn it, for it is freely given. All you have to do is acknowledge it and delight in it.

Does this read like pious froth? Is this kind of thinking a way of escaping from the appalling truths of our world: the oppression, enslavement and genocide? The most passionate and effective women and men I have met in my work for justice and peace are people gifted with a sense of wonder at the preciousness of life. It is because they know this preciousness with their hearts that they react to injustice, oppression and violence with their whole being. They cannot live within the narrow parameters of their individual security, whether it be the security of personal wealth, status, or even of religious respectability. Nor can they tolerate national policies which discriminate against sections of our own nation, nor policies, whether trade agreements or arms sales, which are oppressive to other nations.

When I visited South Africa in 1986, the situation of the Black majority seemed hopeless, for they were dominated by a White regime which bristled with all the modern weaponry of repression. In 1994, I was in South Africa on the day Nelson Mandela was installed as President in a bloodless transfer of power. This transfer was a triumph of the spirit which could never have occurred had there not been thousands of people, Black and White, sustained by faith in a liberating God during the dark years of Apartheid, a faith which is expressed so clearly in their wonderful protest songs.

PRAYER

God, whenever I am feeling hopeless and despondent, let me hear you saying to me, 'The mountains may depart, the hills be shaken, but my love for you will never leave you.'

EXERCISE

After listening in stillness to these words from Isaiah, note what you felt at the time and afterwards, and pray to live in

consciousness that God's Covenant of peace with you will never
be shaken.

Isaiah 49:7–26

> For Zion was saying, 'Yahweh has abandoned me, the
> Lord has forgotten me.' Does a woman forget the baby at
> her breast, or fail to cherish the child of her womb. Yet
> even if these forget, I will never forget you. See I have
> branded you on the palms of my hands. (49:14–16)

This text from Isaiah, like the previous one, was given when
Israel was in exile in Babylon without hope of return; their own
city, Jerusalem, in ruins.

The French thinker, Thoreau, wrote, 'Most men live lives of
quiet desperation.' This generalisation applies, but in different
ways, both to those who engage in the promotion of justice and
peace and to those who dedicate their lives to finding inner peace
and harmony. This different approach to life is to be found among
Christians and often leads to most un-Christian behaviour. The
political and social activists accuse their inactive brothers and
sisters of indulging in selfish navel-gazing, of being content to
pray while the world burns: the prayerful accuse the activists of
lacking true faith. Each faction feels frustrated by the other, and
both suffer feelings of desperation.

Desperation is an emotion charged with promise. If you have
never experienced it, be patient, for it will almost certainly arrive
sooner or later!

Desperation is the result of failed expectations. The more we
have relied on a particular outcome, the more intense is our

feeling of desperation when it does not happen. The activist's vision of a just society is frustrated by the refusal of those in power to change their minds: the prayerful person discovers a God who appears to be deaf to their pleas, and who leaves them in inner turmoil rather than in peace of soul. Neither other people, nor God, nor even ourselves match up to our expectations!

God is in the truth of things, therefore the facts must be kind, however painful I may find them to be. Whatever the facts, God is in them and saying to us, 'I will never forget you. See I have branded you on the palms of my hands.' The pain I feel must be God's nudging me to change in some way, either to change the situation in which I find myself, or the way I am perceiving it. God does not inflict the pain: we inflict much of it on ourselves through our false expectations.

Our false expectations arise from attachment to false securities. If I believe that my ultimate good lies in the accumulation of wealth, achievement, status, good health, or on my notion of spiritual progress, then when these securities are threatened it can feel like annihilation.

'Despair is the last refuge of the ego.' That is why desperation is an emotion charged with promise. It is an invitation to surrender ourselves to the one security we have: our rock, refuge and strength, who has us branded on the palms of his hands.

PRAYER

God, open my eyes so that I can recognise you at work in every detail of my life, however painful, and give me the courage to follow your promptings.

EXERCISE

Look at those things which make you feel desperate. Have we allowed these things to become our idol? Let the words of Isaiah hover over your desperation, 'I will never forget you. See I have branded you on the palms of my hands.'

Wisdom 11:21–12:2

You spare all things because all things are yours, Lord,
lover of life, You whose imperishable spirit is in all.

(11:26)

The book of Wisdom is a late book of the Old Testament, written
about 50 BC, and is the only Old Testament book to be written in
Greek rather than Hebrew, for it is written to let the pagans know
the nature of the God of Israel. In Protestant Bibles the book of
Wisdom appears under 'Apocrypha', because the sixteenth-
century reformers did not accept it as part of the true canon of
Scripture.

In Scripture, God is presented as transcendent – always beyond
the range of human thought or imagining, and yet as immanent –
within all things, 'closer to me than I am to myself'. This passage
from Wisdom contains both these truths: God is transcendent:
'In your sight the whole world is like a grain of dust that tips the
scales', but also immanent: 'You spare all things because all
things are yours, Lord, lover of life, you whose imperishable spirit
is in all.'

The early Christian theologians saw the whole of creation as
sacramental; as a sign, and an effective sign of the presence of
God. The sacraments of the Christian Church are celebrations of
our awareness of the reality of God at all times and to all people.
In Baptism, for example, we celebrate God's continuous invitation
to all creation to be incorporated into the life of God, and in the

Eucharist we celebrate God's continuous self-giving to us in Christ. Every bush is burning, if only we have the eyes to see. Creation itself is sacred, and yet we have managed to forget this, reserving 'the sacred' for our formal religious activities, and considering all else to be 'profane', so that it does not much matter what we do with it. Such an attitude has allowed Christians to destroy peoples and to ravage the environment while still practising their religion.

Because God is transcendent – always greater than anything we can think or imagine – no religion can claim to have an adequate knowledge of God. There has to be a measure of agnosticism in every religious believer.

Because God is immanent – in all things – there is no area of human life in which God is not present. That is why governments with totalitarian leanings, whether they call themselves democratic or are openly military dictatorships, are unable to tolerate religions which raise political, social and economic questions. Those Christian churches or sects which remain silent about the injustice of a regime are, in fact, denying the immanence of God.

PRAYER
God, deepen our faith in you, and save us from betraying you by remaining silent in the face of injustice, whether of the state or of the Church.

EXERCISE
'Religion should keep out of politics.' Reflect on this statement in the light of the Scripture texts you have looked at so far.

Isaiah 43:1–7

> Do not be afraid for I have redeemed you . . . because
> you are precious in my eyes, because you are honoured
> and I love you . . . (43:1, 4)

In Christianity today there is, in general, a split between the
activists on the one hand, and, on the other, those who rely
exclusively on prayer. This is not to deny that there are many
prayerful people who are also active in trying to reform the unjust
structures of society, or that there are a large number of activists
who are prayerful. Christianity demands both prayerfulness and
the active promotion of justice. The inner and outer aspects of
life are a single reality. That is why the Bible places such emphasis
on both prayer and activity.

Today's passage begins with the most common phrase in the
Bible, 'Do not be afraid.' Fear is a very healthy instinct which
enables us to take reasonable care of ourselves, but it can also
become the most destructive force in our lives. Fear is the fuel of
violence. During the Cold War, from 1945 to 1989, western fear
of Russia and Russia's fear of the West led to a nuclear arms race,
in which each side accumulated sufficient weaponry to destroy
all life on earth many times over. Within an individual, fear can
be turned into an inner violence which can paralyse both body
and soul.

Instilling fear is the favoured method of all brainwashers and
tyrants. The Latin poet, Lucretius, writing before the time of

Christ, recognised fear as the most dehumanising of all emotions, and he also saw religion as the most potent source of fear in human beings, because it leads them to act inhumanly towards one another through fear of displeasing the gods who inflict punishment not only in this life but also after death. The Roman emperors recognised the wisdom of Lucretius, so they declared themselves to be divine, thus ensuring tighter control over their subjects!

For many people brought up as Christians, the God with whom they have been presented is a God of judgment, whose main preoccupation seems to be with our sins and their appropriate punishment, both in this world and in the next. Such a God makes life easier for those in charge, whether in Church or state.

In our prayer, it is good to hear God saying to us now, 'Do not be afraid', and to tell God of the things of which we are afraid. Knowing this God in our hearts, we can grow in inner freedom, our energies no longer absorbed in countering our fears and building up our false securities, but released to allow us and others to live.

PRAYER
God, give us the courage to look at our fears, and trusting in you, to befriend them.

EXERCISE
When you do feel afraid of something or someone, ask yourself the question, 'Where is the focus of my attention – on myself, or on God saying "Do not be afraid"?'

Leviticus 25

> Yahweh spoke to Moses . . . Speak to the Israelites and
> say to them . . . Land must not be sold in perpetuity, for
> the land belongs to me, and to me you are only strangers
> and guests. (25:23)

In this chapter of Leviticus, God instructs Moses on the years
which are to be celebrated as Holy Years. Every fiftieth year was
to be celebrated as a year of Jubilee, a year of the Lord's favour.
The word 'Jubilee' comes from the Hebrew 'yobel', meaning a
ram's horn, which was used as a trumpet to announce the
beginning of a year of freedom and reconciliation. In this Jubilee
year slaves were to be set free, property to be returned to its
original owners and debts cancelled. Earlier legislation, in Exodus
21–3, had commanded the liberation of slaves after seven years,
had forbidden the slavery of women, and had ordained that rich
and poor should be treated in the same way before the law, so
that a rich man who had injured the eye of a poor man received
the same injury to his own eye. The legislation in Leviticus is an
adaptation to changing times of the earlier legislation given in
Exodus.

The Jubilee year was a national acknowledgment of the
sovereignty of God over all things and all people, and of the
graciousness and generosity of that sovereignty, 'for the land (and,
we might add, the wealth) belongs to me, and to me you are only
strangers and guests'. Jesus's mission in life was to declare this

sovereignty. At the beginning of his public ministry, he unrolls the scroll and quotes Isaiah:

'The spirit of the Lord is on me, for he has anointed me to bring the good news to the afflicted. He has sent me to proclaim liberty to the captives, sight to the blind, to let the oppressed go free, to proclaim a year of favour from the Lord.' He then rolled up the scroll and said, 'This text is being fulfilled today even while you are listening.'

(Luke 4:17–21)

In our day, whole nations are caught in the poverty trap of national debt, which kills thousands through starvation, because the land, which provided the poor with a subsistence diet, is taken from them, to be used for growing luxury crops, for export to richer nations. The money thus earned helps to pay the interest on massive loans from rich countries for the purchase of arms, or for buildings and other prestige projects which frequently prove useless for Third World needs. Most of these countries will never be able to pay back the capital, so the interest payments must continue indefinitely, leaving no money for development.

Why does this destructive inequality exist? Ultimately, it is because we do not care to do anything about it. Those who could most effectively change things are those who, at present, gain from the inequality.

PRAYER
God, may the nations celebrate the third millennium in the spirit of your year of favour, so that the crushing national debt of poor countries may be cancelled. Deliver us from every form of celebration of the millennium which leaves us undisturbed by the plight of the world's poor.

GOD OF COMPASSION

EXERCISE
Do some reading on the national debt of poorer countries. Leaflets, referring to more detailed accounts, are available from CAFOD and other development agencies. Spread the information wherever you can.

Amos 4:1–3. 5:1–24

I take no pleasure in solemn festivals . . .
But let justice flow like water
and integrity like an unfailing stream. (5:21, 24)

Amos is the earliest of the Old Testament prophets. He lived in the eighth century BC, when Palestine was divided into a northern kingdom, which was prosperous and cultured, and a southern kingdom which was poor and backward. Amos, a shepherd from the south, was called by God to preach to the north. God filled Amos with zeal, but left him short on tact and diplomacy. He addressed the fashionable ladies of Samaria:

'Listen to this word, you cows of Bashan, living in the mountain of Samaria, oppressing the needy, crushing the poor, saying to your husbands, "Bring us something to drink!" The days are coming to you when you will be dragged out with hooks, the very last of you with prongs. Out you will go, each by the nearest breach in the wall, to be driven all the way to Hermon. It is Yahweh who speaks.'

(4:1–3)

One can imagine the comments of the ladies of Samaria. 'How dare this crude upstart disturb us with his socialist rantings? Did you notice that he made no mention of prayer? He obviously has no feel for true religion and spirituality.'

GOD OF COMPASSION

God, through Amos, answers their objections:

> I hate and despise your feasts,
> I take no pleasure in your solemn festivals . . .
> Let me have no more of the din of your chanting,
> no more of your strumming on harps.
> But let justice flow like water,
> and integrity like an unfailing stream. (5:21–4)

God's wrath against Samaria is not because they are failing in their religious observances, for they appear to have had an abundance of them. God, through Amos, is complaining that their observances are not genuine, because their lives are not mirroring God's love and compassion for the poor, whom they are oppressing.

PRAYER
God, give us the grace of integrity so that our love of you, which we express in our religious services, may be manifest in the way we relate to one another.

EXERCISE
These excerpts from Amos put a question mark over our religious services and our lifestyles. Face the question, and talk it over with God, who has compassion on you.

Hosea 11:1–11

'I am the Holy One in your midst and I have no wish to destroy.' (11:9)

Hosea continues the preaching of Amos. Hosea's wife was unfaithful, and this experience enabled him to understand the love of Yahweh for unfaithful Israel. In Hosea, as in all the Hebrew prophets, there are some fearsome threats, for example:

Let her [Israel] rid her face of her whoring . . .
or else I will strip her naked . . .
I will make a wilderness of her,
and turn her into an arid land,
and leave her to die of thirst. (2:2–3)

. . . for Yahweh indicts the citizens of the country:
there is no loyalty, no faithful love,
no knowledge of God in the country,
only perjury and lying, murder and theft,
adultery and violence,
bloodshed after bloodshed.
This is why the country is in mourning
and all its citizens pining away,
the wild animals also and the birds of the sky,
even the fish in the sea will disappear. (4:1–3)

The environment itself is threatened by the wrongdoing. We know the truth of that today.

Yet all these threats are uttered in order to win back Israel:

That is why I am going to block her way with thorns,
and wall her in so that she cannot find her way;
she will chase after her lovers and never catch up with them,
she will search for them and never find them.
Then she will say,
'I will go back to my first husband,
I was happier then than I am today.' (2:6–7)

Israel, come back to Yahweh your God
your guilt was the cause of your downfall . . .
I shall cure them of their disloyalty,
I shall love them with all my heart . . .
I shall fall like dew on Israel,
he will bloom like the lily . . .
and thrust out roots . . .
like the cedar of Lebanon. (14:1, 5–6)

PRAYER
God, enlighten our minds so that acknowledging our wrongdoing, we may glimpse the depths of your goodness in forgiving us, and so long for you with our entire being.

EXERCISE
Read the prophet Hosea for yourself and note how all the wrathful passages are the obverse of God's love for Israel.

Isaiah 24

The earth is mourning, withering,
the world is pining, withering,
the heavens are pining away with the earth. (Isaiah 24:4)

Having read this text, you may be groaning within and asking,
'Why can't he choose a cheerful passage for a change?' But there
is a way of looking at this and similar passages which, far from
plunging us into deeper gloom, can offer us hope.

This chapter of Isaiah which begins 'See how Yahweh lays
the earth waste, makes it a desert, buckles its surface',
becomes progressively more threatening until verse 19, when
'The earth will split into fragments, the earth will be riven
and rent, the earth will shiver and shake . . . it will fall never
to rise again.'

What is behind all the threats? 'For they have transgressed the
law, violated the precept, broken the everlasting covenant.' (v.45)

The Bible, as we have already seen, assumes a close interconnection between the behaviour of human beings and the
wellbeing of nature, the plants, rivers, animals, and the climate,
so that evil within the human heart destroys not only the
individual, but the very earth. If this assumption seems to us
primitive and quaint, we need only reflect on some of the
outstanding disasters of our own century to see how the ambitions
of individuals have brought misery and death to millions, how
the greed of a few, with the collusion of many, has plundered the

47

earth's natural resources, threatening the survival of future generations.

The evil in our hearts can create much more damage than we realise, affecting nature itself. We are unaware of the close interconnection between ourselves and the whole of creation. Our personhood is something which extends beyond the range of our conscious minds. What subject interests you most? On what subject do you consider yourself most ignorant? The answer to both questions is the same: myself! Our unending curiosity about our own identity is very healthy. We suspect that there may be more to us than our conscious mind presents. We are far more than our *Curriculum Vitae*. Our soul expresses itself through our body, but is not limited within the confines of our body. Being spirit, our soul cannot be contained even within the whole of creation. All creation is held in unity by God, the heart of the universe. In opening our hearts to God and in letting God's compassion take hold on us in the ways in which we relate to others and to the world around us, we can bring life to people and to nature in ways our conscious minds may never grasp this side of death.

For the Christian, despondency is a serious sin, for it is a denial of the truth that God, in Christ, has entered into our sinfulness and into our death, is risen again, and dwells within and around us.

PRAYER

God, never let us abandon the peace which you offer us, a peace which nothing can shatter, not even death itself.

EXERCISE

Reflect for yourself on some of the disasters which have befallen us in this century and which were brought about by human decisions.

Isaiah 10

Woe to the legislators of infamous laws,
to those who issue tyrannical decrees,
and who refuse justice to the unfortunate
and cheat the poor among my people of their rights,
who make widows their prey
and rob the orphan. (10:1–2)

It is astonishing that in spite of the clear prophetic message that Yahweh is a God of compassion for all creation, a God of mercy and of justice, many Christians can still consider the promotion of social, economic and political justice to be extraneous to religion, as though these issues were a contamination of true spirituality. Archbishop Helder Camara of Recife, in Brazil, said, 'When I give bread to a poor man, they call me a saint. When I ask why he has no bread, they call me a Communist.' The easiest way to grasp this truth is to imagine yourself and your family to be utterly destitute, without money or shelter, through no fault of your own. You have been ruined by the greed of others, who have worked the law to their own advantage. You take the family to church and explain your plight. The congregation are not interested and have you thrown out, so that they can continue with their devotions in peace. This is the kind of situation which the prophet Isaiah is addressing.

This separation of ordinary life from religion has its advantages: it keeps God from interfering with our self-interest, whether as individuals, groups or nations. For this reason politicians can be especially vehement on the need to keep religion out of politics, but they are not the only culprits: we all do it.

Our attitude to law is an example of this tendency. In St John's Passion account, the crowds answer Pilate: 'We have a Law, and according to that Law he ought to die.' This answer echoes down the centuries to our own times. The defence given by war criminals, for example, is almost invariably, 'We were obeying orders', as though obedience to law and order excuses any kind of behaviour. Churches can be as guilty as the state in treating law as though it were an absolute, which is to turn law and order into an idol.

Laws exist in order to enable us to live with the maximum freedom compatible with the freedom of others. On the most solemn law of observing the Sabbath, Jesus said, 'The Sabbath is made for human beings, not human beings for the Sabbath.' When laws oppress individuals or groups in society, then it is our duty to disobey: for that is the Law of the Covenant!

PRAYER

God, free us from that spirit of conformity to law, authority and convention, which leads us to find our security in these things rather than in you.

EXERCISE

In life, how often do I act on 'oughts'? Where are the 'oughts' coming from? From fear of losing the approval of other people, or from fear of not letting God be the God of compassion to me and through me?

Isaiah 31:1–9

Woe to those who go down to Egypt to seek help there,
and who build their hopes on cavalry...
and on the strength of mounted men
but never look to the holy One of Israel
nor consult Yahweh. (31:1)

Some of the Old Testament prophets had such trust in God that they opposed the people's request for a king, a request which they saw as a lack of faith in Yahweh's leadership. In this passage, Isaiah warns Israel against thinking that they can defend themselves by making foreign alliances with other military powers. Israel can only find security by turning back to God: 'so will Yahweh Sabaoth protect Jerusalem' (31:5). This preaching did not make the prophets popular, especially with the military.

Have you heard the story of the man hanging on to a branch on the edge of a cliff? He cries out, 'Is there anyone up there?' A voice replies, 'Trust me and let go.' 'Who are you?' asks the man. 'I am God' is the reply. To which the man shouts, 'Is there anybody else up there?'

We are all like the man on the cliff-edge. For our national security, for what we are pleased to call our freedom and our national values, we endorse a nuclear defence policy. No political party in Britain stands a chance of election unless it supports such a policy. It is as though we are saying to God, 'We shall praise, reverence and thank you in our religious services, but please do not interfere in our national defence and foreign policies.'

Is the prophetic message in today's reading hopelessly idealistic and utterly impractical for us today? If we believe that it is, then we should admit this to ourselves, declare it openly, and be prepared to live with the consequences of that admission.

If we believe that God's message is practical, how are we to live it? Real change within society has to begin within individuals, or it will not happen at all. In the past, the legal abolition of slavery was thought to be impossible. We need to work and to pray more for the outlawing of nuclear weapons and for the abolition of the arms trade.

PRAYER

God, teach us that we have no ultimate defence in this world except in your Spirit, the source of our freedom.

EXERCISE

Sit before God and lay out all your worries and anxieties before him. How far do these anxieties dominate your life, forcing you to build up defences against loss of possessions, status, etc? Hand over your anxieties to God. In this way, our anxieties can lead us to a deeper faith in the reality of God.

Micah 6:1–8

This is what Yahweh asks of you:
only this, to act justly, to love tenderly,
and to walk humbly with your God. (6:8)

Many countries are becoming increasingly conscious of their rights. It is important that we should know them, claim them and protest against their violation on our own and others' behalf. There are, however, disadvantages in our rights' consciousness. We can become so absorbed in the question of our individual rights that we ignore the corollary of our rights: our duties.

In this passage from Micah, God says nothing about our rights, but concentrates on our duties. The advantage of this approach is that we see our rights in clearer perspective, and are less likely to spend all our energy in battling against our opponents, whether real or imaginary.

Act justly. What exactly does that mean? I don't know, but to treat others as we would have them treat us is a very good guideline in all our dealings. The guideline is simple, but to live it requires imagination and an ability to take a leap out of our own conditioning into the mind and conditioning of the other. If we can do this, we then discover our own unwillingness to change, and so reach the roots of injustice in ourselves. The most important and effective work any of us can do for the promotion of justice is to start on the roots of injustice within ourselves.

Love tenderly. Do you ever feel your life is blighted because you have never been sufficiently loved? You may feel that you have been overlooked, slighted, insulted, rejected, betrayed. Such experiences can destroy all our interest in and enjoyment of life, whether the rejection is real or imagined. If we can turn our attention to our need to love, ignoring the fact that we feel that we ourselves are unloved, the effect can be amazing and we can find a great load falling from us.

Walk humbly before your God. Humility derives from the Latin word 'humus' meaning the earth. Humility is about seeing the truth of things, seeing ourselves in perspective, so that we are no longer the centre of the universe, but an element in its dance, with God as the choreographer. It is also the virtue which enables us to laugh, for it makes us more able to see the ridiculousness of our own behaviour and that of other people.

PRAYER
God, show me your attractiveness, so that my heart is set on you and on your kingdom of justice, tenderness and truth.

EXERCISE
Reflect on this saying: 'Wisdom is to know the harmony of things, and joy is to dance to its rhythm.' Micah explains the steps of the dance: to act justly, love tenderly, to walk humbly before God.

Luke 1:26–56

> 'I am the handmaid of the Lord,' said Mary. 'Let what
> you have said be done to me.' (1:38)

In his *Spiritual Exercises*, the sixteenth-century Basque noble-
man, Ignatius Loyola, who became the founder of the Society of
Jesus, or Jesuits, as they were later called, proposes an imaginative
contemplation on the Incarnation. Ignatius imagines the Trinity
looking down on the world and its peoples, 'some black, some
white, some at peace, some at war, some weeping, some laughing,
some healthy, others sick, some being born, others dying', and
then he adds, 'see how human beings are destroying themselves'.
This is a good image to work with. Watch the delicate globe of
our world as it appears from space. See it slowly revolving and,
like a camera lens, zoom in on any part of it.

What does God do in the face of our destructiveness? The
sensible thing would surely have been to convert the Emperor
Augustus, ruler of the known world at the time of Christ, but God
sends an angel to an unknown girl in an obscure and troublesome
outpost of the Roman Empire and asks the impossible of her,
putting her life at risk. She is to conceive a child without a human
father. The punishment for adultery was stoning to death and she
is already engaged to a man called Joseph, so God's arrangement
would, at the very least, disrupt the relationship. Mary is terrified
at first and cannot understand how she can do what is being asked
of her. She ends the interview with 'Behold the handmaid of the

Lord, let what you have said be done to me.' It is as though nature awaits her answer with bated breath, for on her answer depends the future of all peoples and all things.

God's Covenant is with all creation, but the Covenant is revealed to individuals and invites their co-operation. In his poem 'The Blessed Virgin compared to the air we breathe', Gerard Manley Hopkins says of Mary:

> This one work has to do –
> Let all God's glory through,
> God's glory which would go
> Through her and from her flow . . .

To bring God to birth is the task of every Christian. As St Paul prays, 'May Christ live in your hearts through faith . . . for his power working in us can do infinitely more than we can ask or imagine' (Ephesians 3:17, 20).

PRAYER

Lord, through the message of an angel, your Word took flesh in the womb of the Virgin Mary. Open our hearts to receive your word, so that Christ may live in our hearts and be revealed in our lives.

EXERCISE

In imagination, have a conversation with Mary after she has received the angel's message. Then say to God, 'Open my mind to glimpse the wonder of my being and my call, so that I can let all your glory through.'

Luke 2:1–20

She wrapped him in swaddling clothes, and laid him in a
manger because there was no room for them at the inn.

(2:7)

When I first met my friend, Donald Nicholl, after he had been
told that he had terminal cancer, he said to me, 'I've been
thinking. I think that thinking is part of the punishment for the
Fall, so I have given up thinking and spend my days in gazing.'

Gazing is a most profitable occupation, for in gazing, instead
of controlling our thinking and feeling, we allow thoughts and
feelings to arise in us. For example, in gazing at a landscape,
we may find ourselves at peace and delighting in the beauty
and spaciousness of the scene. This experience of peace and
delight may make us more aware of the lack of peace in our
normal way of life. Gazing has deepened our awareness and so
raised questions of fundamental importance for our wellbeing,
questions which we are normally too busy or too afraid to
consider.

Gazing is another word for contemplating, and it is through
contemplation that we can come into contact with the reality of
God, who dreams within us, the God of all creation. In the
introduction I wrote that studying the Bible and praying the
Bible are two different activities. Contemplating Bible passages
can open us up to the reality of God so that the Word can
transform us, instead of our trying to transform the Word of

57

God to fit our ready made thought patterns.

In this reading, imagine the scene happening at this moment and that you are present in it. See the child in the manger, Mary, Joseph, and yourself, allowing your imagination to supply any other details. Just gaze at the scene and see what happens. You don't have to force anything, just be there. If you feel prompted to talk with Mary and Joseph, to ask them if you may hold the child, then do so. Talk to them about their lives and about your own.

In St Paul's words, this child is 'the image of the God we cannot see'. Whenever we look at Jesus in the Gospels, there is a sense in which we are looking at a self-portrait, for the whole object of our lives as Christians is that 'Christ may live in your hearts through faith, and then, planted in love and built on love . . . so that knowing the love of Christ, which is beyond knowledge, you may be filled with the utter fullness of God' (Ephesians 3:17–19).

God is with us. In everyone we encounter, God is. 'As you do to one another, you are doing also to me.' We are meeting God in all our encounters, not just at church services.

PRAYER
God, still our hearts and minds so that we can learn to gaze, and through gazing glimpse you, our soul's desiring.

EXERCISE
There are millions of children today for whom there is no room anywhere, no food, no water, not because these necessities are unavailable, but because other human beings refuse to make them available. Speak to Jesus about this. He identifies himself with each of them. Ask him what you can do.

Matthew 2:1–23

'Get up. Take the child and his mother with you, and
escape into Egypt.' (2:13)

We read the Scripture in order to understand the present, for God,
who became one of us in Jesus, is God holding us in being at this
moment. This passage of Scripture can enlighten us about many
aspects of life today. This one affects every believer in God.

If you have never said, 'How could God let this happen to
me?', you have very probably asked 'How could God allow this
to happen to them?' The problem of evil is one of the greatest
barriers to belief.

Our difficulties with belief in an all-powerful God who permits
the existence of evil spring from our assumptions about the nature
of God. In our prayer we address God as, 'Almighty, all-powerful
God', assuming that God's ideas of might and power are the same
as our own. If I were almighty and all-powerful, then I should get
rid of all this evil at once, so why does God fail to do so?

'Take the child and his mother with you and escape into Egypt.'
Why does God allow this? Why not eliminate Herod before he
started on the massacre? But the child and his parents have to
become refugees and are powerless against the might of Herod.

It seems, then, as though trust in God provides no protection
against tyrants, oppressors, exploiters; as though God is powerless
against the powers of this world. This refugee child, when he
grows up, will be tempted to exercise power and control over the

59

powers of this world by assuming supreme power himself, but he will reject the temptation, because this is not the way of God. Here we touch on the heart of the matter. When St John describes God, he does not say 'God is power', but 'God is love.' In what sense, therefore, can we call God our protector, our refuge, our strength?

We are created for something far greater that the exercise of power over one another. We are created for one another, not against one another. We are created for co-operation instead of competition, to be life-giving rather than life-destroying, for love, not hate. 'Love,' as St Paul says, 'is always patient and kind, love is never jealous ... it is never rude and never seeks its own advantage, it does not take offence or store up grievances', and it is stronger than death.

PRAYER
God, change my mind and heart, so that in all my relations with others I try to co-operate rather than compete, and see my good as inseparable from theirs.

EXERCISE
What do you most want in life? To control as many people as possible, or to co-operate with as many as possible? Then choose the path which brings you life.

Luke 2:41–52

> 'Did you not know that I must be busy with my Father's
> affairs?' But they did not understand what he meant.
>
> (2:49)

Luke is the only evangelist who gives us a direct quotation from
the words of Jesus during the first thirty years of his life. On a
trip to Jerusalem at the age of twelve Jesus goes missing and his
parents don't catch up with him until three days later, when he
gives this reply, leaving them baffled.

St Paul tells us that Luke was a doctor, but he is also said to
have been an artist. He is certainly a prose artist, for in this one
phrase he sums up the essence of Jesus's life, his relationship to
his Father, whom he later addresses as 'Abba', corresponding to
our 'Dad' or 'Daddy'.

Whenever we read of Jesus in the Gospels, we are also reading
our own autobiography, our own destiny, because 'Before the
world was made, God chose us, chose us in Christ, to live in love
in his presence' (Ephesians 1:4). Doing the will of the Father is
the underlying theme of all of Jesus's life and teaching,
culminating in his agony in the garden when he prays 'Not my
will but Thine be done', and on the cross when he prays 'Into Thy
hands I commend my spirit.'

Consequently, 'doing the Father's will' must be the underlying
theme of our lives, but what does this mean? Other people,
religious people especially, are only too glad to tell us. According

to many of them, doing the Father's will mean renouncing our own will and doing whatever these religious authorities tell us, which is the reason why so many decide that religion is not for them.

'God is closer to me than I am to myself.' To find God's will, look into your own heart. What do you really desire from life? This is not an easy question to answer, but it is important to keep asking, for the closer we come to an answer, the nearer we are to discovering the will of God. The answer to the question is within you. You will know when you are approaching the right answer, for you will find that you are enjoying life more, that you are less anxious, more interested in all around you and more compassionate, because you are beginning 'to live in love in his presence'.

There is a medieval painting of the finding of the child Jesus in the Temple. Jesus is looking stroppy, Mary angry, and Joseph despairing. Contemplate this scene and be present in it with them. Ask them about their difficulties with one another and tell them of your own!

PRAYER
God, from whom we come, to whom we go, teach me to listen to my own heart, in which you live. Teach me to recognise you in the hearts of those I meet.

EXERCISE
Make out a list of your desires. You will find many are incompatible, for example, 'I desire to be truthful, but I also want to be popular.' Struggle with your list until you find what you really desire above all else. And revise your findings frequently, for our deepest desire is not usually on the surface of our consciousness.

Matthew 3:13–17

'This is my Son, the Beloved: my favour rests on him.'

(3:17)

These few verses of Matthew describe Jesus leaving home to begin his public life. After being baptised by John, 'He saw the Spirit of God descending like a dove and coming down on him. And a voice spoke from heaven, "This is my Son, the Beloved: my favour rests on him."'

When asked to introduce yourself to a group of people, how do you identify yourself after giving your name? I am a businessman, a housewife, a doctor, a baker? And if you are unemployed, or unable to work, how do you feel about declaring this? Because we identify ourselves by what we do, we feel devastated when we are no longer capable of doing it, as though we had lost our very being.

You are not your occupation, you are not your achievements, you are not your failings, nor your health, wealth or status. All these things are connected with you, but are not you, for you do not cease to exist when these things disappear. Ultimately, who are you?

Our conscious minds can grasp only the tiniest fraction of the reality in which we are living. Scripture is constantly telling us this. We are puny creatures, living for a blink of time, on a journey from dust to dust. Yet we are also made in the image of God, who identifies his very self with each one of us, 'As you do to one of these least, you are doing also to me.' Jesus said, 'I am in my Father, and you are in me, and I am in you' (John 14:20).

Who are you? You are a unique manifestation of God, who is closer to you than you are to yourself. This is the truth of your being, the glory and the wonder of it. Contemplate this passage. In imagination, talk to Jesus after his baptism. Go down to the Jordan yourself, be baptised by John and hear God say, 'You are my beloved, my favour rests on you.' If this suggestion seems to you to be an illegitimate use of the Gospel, recall St Paul's words to the Ephesians: 'Before the world was, he formed us, formed us in Christ, to live in love in his presence.'

PRAYER

God, change my way of seeing, so that in every experience I can recognise you beckoning me to be at one with you and with all creation.

EXERCISE

After listening to these words of God, 'You are my beloved, my favour rests on you', notice your reactions. Disbelief, embarrassment, 'Yes but . . . ?' And reflect on how your life would be if you could really believe this. What would happen to most of your worries and judgments, the values you hold about yourself and other people?

Matthew 4:1–11

'You must worship the Lord your God, and serve him alone.' (4:10)

When people ask what I do and I answer 'I work in spirituality', the usual response is 'how interesting', before moving on to much more interesting topics like the weather. Spirituality is a vague word, hard to define, but it concerns our perception of life. The way in which we act and react depends on our way of perceiving, thus spirituality can get to the roots of human life, the sources of our happiness and sadness, our creativity and destructiveness. How are we to distinguish between what is life-giving and what is destructive in human life?

The Roman emperors had a very effective way of controlling their vast empire. The policy was, 'Give the people bread and provide them with circuses.' A people well-fed and entertained are less likely to prove troublesome. In order to exercise complete control, the emperors declared themselves to be divine, so that displeasing the emperor in this life would also lead to punishment after death, a very effective deterrent to disobedience!

Jesus is tempted to turn stones into bread, to leap off the pinnacle of the Temple, the equivalent of a circus act, and finally he is tempted to take control of everything in the world. Jesus rejects each temptation by referring it to God. 'Human beings do not live by bread alone, but by every word which comes from the mouth of God'; 'Thou shalt not tempt the Lord, your God'; 'You must worship the Lord Your God, and serve him alone.'

The temptations seem very reasonable and plausible. Why not turn stones into bread, not, of course, merely to satisfy one's own hunger after a forty-day fast, but also to be able to supply bread for the hungry of the world? Why not put on a dramatic show for the crowds by a leap from the Temple? It could bring people to their senses and make them more attentive to God's Word. And why not take control of everything in the world, ensuring sound and just government, putting an end to war, poverty and oppression.

Briefly, all the temptations are temptations to idolatry, to dedicate one's whole being to some created thing; riches, power, the exercise of control. Wealth, health, honour, status and power to control are not wrong in themselves. We need wealth, which is a form of energy, and human society cannot be organised without some measure of control, but when these things become ends in themselves, they destroy us.

PRAYER

Lord, give me such a longing for you and for your ways that I can never cling to anyone, or anything, as though it was my ultimate security.

EXERCISE

The roots of all violence are to be found in these temptations. To unearth these roots in ourselves, ask yourself, 'What gets me het up, whether in rage or with delight?' Then listen to that phrase, 'You must serve God alone.'

Luke 4:16–30

He has sent me to bring the good news to the poor,
to proclaim liberty to captives . . .
to set the downtrodden free
to proclaim the Lord's year of favour. (4:18)

After the temptation, Jesus returns to Nazareth and preaches in the synagogue, quoting the above verses from Isaiah and declaring, 'This text is being fulfilled today, even as you listen.' The congregation approve at first and are impressed with Jesus's words, but when he goes on to explain that God's favour is not limited to the Jews, but extends to the pagans, their approval changes to indignation and they try to throw him over a cliff-edge.

Why the sudden change in the congregation's mood? They are quite happy to hear these words of Isaiah applied to themselves, but are not happy to think that these words can be applied to the pagans as well. They do not consider such 'inclusiveness' to be good news, a liberation, a sign of God's generosity, because it now includes strangers.

This reaction reveals a fundamental flaw in human nature. We tend to identify ourselves by the ways in which we differ from other people and not in co-operation with them. 'I am different, therefore I am.' Yes, we are all different, with different finger-prints, different cell-prints; but our many differences form us into the one Body of Christ.

Believing that our identity lies in our being different from others, we then strive to emphasise those differences. We see those who are different as a threat, so we try to overcome them, subdue or eliminate them. That is why we have a world threatened with extinction because of our militarism, racism, sexism, and our religious and ideological differences. Jesus's mission is to deliver us from the captivity and misery which this way of thinking imposes on us.

The implications of the cosmic nature of God's Covenant are enormous. Think, for example, how it can change our understanding of evangelism. The former Secretary of the Church Missionary Society, Canon Max Warren, once wrote, 'Whenever you meet another person, of another culture, another faith, or of no faith, take off your shoes, for you are entering holy ground, and tread warily, for God has been there before you.'

All the people I meet, who are engaged in multi-faith work, claim that their knowledge and insight into other faiths has helped them better to appreciate the breadth and depth of their own faith. This is not surprising, if God's Covenant is with all peoples.

PRAYER
God, give us the grace of learning how to listen so that we can recognise that which is of you in everyone, however different they may be from ourselves.

EXERCISE
In light of God's Cosmic Covenant, reflect on this Buddhist saying: 'The bodhisatva does not desire nirvana (heaven), until the last blade of grass has achieved enlightenment!'

John 1:35–39

> Jesus said, 'What do you want?' They answered, 'Rabbi, where do you live?' 'Come and see' he replied; so they went and saw where he lived, and stayed with him the rest of that day. (1:38–39)

John the Baptist, standing by the Jordan, sees Jesus passing and says to two of his own disciples, 'Look, there is the Lamb of God.' The two disciples follow Jesus, who asks them, 'What do you want?'

It is good to contemplate this passage again and again, hearing Jesus asking us, 'What do you want?', then talking to him about what we do really want. It is a heart-searching question, for if we try to answer it, we become aware of our multiple and conflicting desires. We also come to realise that the whole direction and quality of our lives depends upon the way in which we cope with our desires. 'Each is led by her/his own desire,' wrote the poet, Virgil, so it is very important for us to discover what we really desire.

The advertising industry is based on the fact that desire determines the way in which we act and react. Advertisers fuel consumerism by convincing us of the desirability of their products, thus contributing to excessive consumption of the world's resources by the wealthier nations, while the poor starve and the whole planet is threatened as the consumer nations poison the atmosphere with their noxious fumes.

When the Gerasene demoniac was asked by Jesus, 'What is your name?', he answered with great insight, 'My name is legion, because there are many of us.' When Jesus asks us 'What do you want?', we begin to see something of the demoniac in ourselves, for we become aware of our many and conflicting desires. We want to be popular and to be loved, but we also want to be truthful: we cannot always be both. We want to be open-minded, but we are also unwilling to change.

Our desire for trivialities, for instant gratification, is usually more insistent than our deeper desire to be true, generous, loving and compassionate. If we always follow the more insistent desire, then we tear ourselves and others apart: we feel frustrated and blame everyone except ourselves. That is why this question, 'What do you want?' is so important and why we need to keep listening to it.

PRAYER
God, enlighten our minds and hearts so that we can come to know you, our heart's desiring.

EXERCISE
Imagine you have died and someone writes your obituary notice. Write the obituary yourself, not the one you are afraid you might receive, but the one which you would love to have in your wildest dreams, not allowing reality to limit you in the slightest! This exercise can help us discover what we really want.

Luke 6:20–45

'Be compassionate as your Father is compassionate.'
(Luke 6:36)

In the Covenant, God commits himself to us and calls us to commit ourselves to him, 'Be holy, as I the Lord, your God am holy.' In the Sermon on the Mount, the Christian manifesto, Jesus draws out the implications of this Covenant, the way in which we are to mirror the goodness of God in all our relationships with others.

'But I say this to those of you who are listening: Love your enemies, do good to those who hate you . . . To the person who slaps you on one cheek, present the other cheek too; to the person who takes your cloak from you, do not refuse your tunic.'

We have reached the heart of the matter, the heart of the Covenant. It is extraordinary how much time, energy and money we can spend in building up the body of the Church while ignoring its heart. We can live and act like dedicated undertakers! Chesterton's declaration, 'It is not that Christianity has been tried and found wanting: it has not been tried', is most vividly illustrated in Jesus's Sermon on the Mount.

Part of the reason for our failure to emphasise this central teaching of Jesus is that we misinterpret it, as though in order to be a follower of Jesus we have to model ourselves on a doormat. Among the Jews, the mark of utter contempt was to strike another on the face with the back of one's right hand. If the victim turns

71

the other cheek, the aggressor will find it very difficult to strike again. If the victim does not threaten, but turns the other cheek, the aggressor's violence is lessened, for violence is fuelled by fear. The unthreatening reaction of the victim may, in fact, bring the aggressor to their senses. Similarly, in the advice, 'Give your tunic as well', Jesus is saying, 'Resist in such a way that your aggressors are brought to their senses and no one is harmed.' The context of this advice is a law court. As the victim's tunic is all that he is wearing, he stands naked in court before his creditors.

The action is a benevolent shock tactic, revealing to the aggressor the consequences of his action.

Jesus does not say that we are to collude with evil: we must resist it, but we must resist in love and without doing violence to our enemies, for that is the way of God, 'who lets his rain fall on the just and the unjust alike'. We are to act in this way because this is the way of God. 'Be compassionate, as your Father is compassionate.' And God, in Jesus, did not resist violently, but allowed himself to be stripped and nailed to a cross.

PRAYER

God, may your Spirit of gentleness and compassion so possess us that all our work for peace and justice is done with love for the oppressor as well as for the oppressed.

EXERCISE

Reflect on the phrase 'a disarming manner', and recall examples of non-violent resistance that you have experienced, or heard about.

Matthew 5:1–48

'How happy are the poor in spirit:
theirs is the kingdom of heaven.' (5:3)

The Greeks had many words for happiness. The highest form of happiness was to be *makarios*, a word reserved for the virtuous dead living on the islands of the blest. To be makarios was to have achieved a state of happiness which nothing could shatter, not even death itself. In Matthew's Gospel, the word we translate as 'happy' is this word makarios.

Just before writing this, I was reading a new year message in the *Guardian*, in which an English bishop complained of the spiritual poverty of modern Britain. Obviously, we have a problem with vocabulary: the bishop deplores what St Matthew proposes as an ideal!

In the Gospel, poverty of spirit indicates an inner disposition of total trust in God in all things and in all circumstances. St Paul exemplifies this inner disposition when he writes, 'I have learned to manage on what I have. I know how to be poor and I know how to be rich too . . . now I am ready for anything anywhere: full stomach or empty stomach, poverty or plenty. There is nothing I cannot master with the help of the One who gives me strength' (Philippians 4:12–14). If we really possessed this degree of trust, we could, for example, face public criticism of our failings and sins, thank the critics for their contribution to truth and feel nothing but goodwill towards them!

When the bishop deplores the spiritual poverty of modern Britain he is using the phrase in the opposite sense to St Matthew. The bishop is deploring an inner disposition which is totally dependent on possessing plenty and which is miserable when deprived of having even more. This inner disposition is the root cause of all human violence and injustice. It is destructive of the poor, and, ultimately, of the rich, too.

Poverty of spirit in St Paul's sense means utter freedom. Because his heart is Christ-centred, and Christ is, for Paul, Lord of all creation, there is 'nothing which can come between us and the love of Christ, even if we are worried or troubled, or being persecuted, or lacking food or clothes, or being threatened or even attacked' (Romans 8:35). If we possessed this poverty of spirit, we could delight fully in people and in things, because our enjoyment would not be marred by our fears of losing them.

PRAYER

God, show me the attractiveness of your face, so that drawn by you, I may learn how to delight in your creation without being possessed by it.

EXERCISE

Return to your basic desire again. Which inner disposition would you most like to have: St Paul's, or that which the bishop describes as the inner disposition of modern Britain?

Matthew 13:4–32

> 'The kingdom of heaven is like the yeast a woman took
> and mixed in with three measures of flour till it was
> leavened all through.' (13:33)

This series of parables illustrates the meaning of 'the Kingdom
of Heaven', and the way it relates to our everyday life.

A few years ago someone taught me to make bread. When the
hot water and brown sugar were poured into a glass containing
the hard grains of yeast, the yeast dissolved and the whole mixture
began to froth, looking like a glass of Guinness. This part of the
process corresponds to our own inner experience of enthusiasm
for some venture: we bubble over with plans and excitement.

Then the liquid mixture is poured gradually into the bowl of
flour and the kneading begins. This corresponds to putting our
plans into action. The initial enthusiasm begins to wane. The
grains of flour show a marked disinclination to get mixed up
with the yeast, and they keep escaping up the side of the bowl.
This corresponds to our innate reluctance to change in any way:
we prefer to remain as we are. In carrying out any plan which
began with enthusiasm, we soon come up against our own inertia.
In bread-baking the yeast mixture has to be poured in gradually,
and the flour kneaded, until it has permeated the whole mass.

When putting our decisions into practice, we run the risk of
abandoning the project once the laborious process of kneading
begins, unless our motivation – the yeast mixture – is sufficiently

strong. We need to keep reverting to that initial motivation, otherwise we shall never persist in carrying through our dream. That is why regular prayer is so important in Christian life; prayer which comes from our heart, from our basic desire to let God be God to us and through us.

PRAYER
God, work on my heart so that a longing for you and for your Kingdom so infatuates me that it overrides my surface desires for my kingdom of financial security, personal health, status and self-importance.

EXERCISE
This is a simple exercise which can be done towards the end of each day. First, recall those moments of the day which you have enjoyed, relish them and thank God for them. Those moments are God's gift, signs of God's self-giving to you.

Then pray for enlightenment, so that you can recognise God at work in you. Look first at your moods and feelings during the day, but without any judging or moralising. Then ask yourself, 'What were the desires underlying my moods? Was it desire for my personal kingdom of wealth, status, etc., or was it desire for God's Kingdom of truth, justice, peace and compassion?

Luke 15:1–32

The tax collectors and the sinners, meanwhile, were all
seeking his company. The Pharisees and the scribes
complained, 'This man', they said 'welcomes sinners and
eats with them.' (15:1–3)

What is God like, this God of the Covenant? In the rest of this
chapter St Luke gives three parables describing the nature of
God: the parables of the lost sheep, the lost drachma, and the two
sons who are lost in their different ways – the prodigal and his
dutiful brother. All three parables emphasise God's special love
for the stray, the outcast and the 'hopeless case'.

'He welcomes sinners and eats with them.' This was a cause of
scandal in Jesus's time: it is still a cause of scandal today. The
permissive society which, as the bishop complained, is poor in
spirituality, can still outdo the Pharisees in self-righteous
condemnation. We love and relish condemnation both of
individuals and of groups. The more our newspapers indulge in
condemnation and give us the lurid details of the wrongdoing of
an individual or group, the better their sales. Condemnation of
another can help us to feel safe, and the louder our condemnation,
the more self-righteous we can feel. I often wonder whether Adolf
Hitler did not comfort himself with the thought that he was tee-
total, vegetarian and a non-smoker!

Jesus does not condemn: 'Do not condemn and you will not
be condemned' (Luke 6:37): he welcomes and seems to enjoy the

company of society's outcasts. God's ways are not our ways, God's thoughts are not our thoughts. Jesus illustrates this most clearly in another parable; that of the Pharisee and the tax collector who both go to the Temple to pray. The Pharisee thanks God for making him so virtuous and not like the tax collector. The tax collector prays, 'Lord, have mercy on me a sinner.' And Jesus says that it was the tax collector and not the Pharisee who left the Temple in a right relationship with God.

What is important in God's eyes is not our achievements, our virtue, our respectability, our failures, our past sins: what is all important is that we recognise in our hearts our total dependence on God.

PRAYER

God, give us by grace a true knowledge of ourselves, so that we may never condemn others, but always mirror your gentleness and readiness to forgive. Help us to know that you have forgiven us for the damage we have done, and that you have protected us from doing greater evil.

EXERCISE

Imaginatively contemplate the parable of the two sons in Luke, Chapter 15. Both sons – the prodigal and the self-righteous – are in each of us.

Luke 16:19–31

'If they will not listen either to Moses or the prophets, they will not be convinced even if someone should rise again from the dead.' (16:31)

These verses conclude Jesus's parable of Dives and Lazarus. The wealthy Dives, having failed to notice the impoverished Lazarus starving at his gate, finds himself in torment in Hades after death, while Lazarus is in Abraham's bosom. Dives begs Abraham to let his brothers know the fate that awaits them for ignoring the poor. Abraham refuses, 'If they will not listen either to Moses or the prophets . . .'

'Be holy, as I the Lord your God am holy.' The parables reveal Jesus's understanding of the meaning of the holiness of God. St Paul says, 'Let that mind be in you which is also in Christ Jesus.' That is why the parables are so important.

The parable of Dives and Lazarus is very disturbing. There is no suggestion that Dives persecutes or oppresses Lazarus. Dives may well have been a believer in the Gospel of Prosperity, thanking God for the many blessings bestowed on him. He might even have held prayer meetings in his mansion. Dives simply does not notice Lazarus, and it is his failure to notice which brings him to torment in Hades. If we think that this is a very unfair punishment, it is worth pondering our reaction.

Why do I think the punishment unfair? Because Dives has not deliberately wronged Lazarus? Here we come up against the difference between our thinking and God's thinking. We see ourselves as individuals struggling to live as best we can. The effort to do so can so preoccupy us that we simply do not notice what is happening to others. One political party promises a reduction in taxes, while the opposition threatens to raise them, so why not vote for the party offering the tax cut?

Jesus's thinking is different. He thinks not in terms of 'me', but of 'us', and 'us' includes all human beings. What glorious breadth of thinking, and how very awkward for those of us whose security depends upon our ability to ignore the plight of others. The gap between the rich and poor of the world is widening rapidly, not primarily because of lack of resources, but because of their unfair distribution.

PRAYER
God, change my thinking and my way of perceiving, so that instead of wanting all creation to centre around me, I see my good as service of you and your creation.

EXERCISE
Reflect on the parameters of our own decisions. In so many institutions and businesses today, whether of Church or state, the ultimate criterion of all decision-making is money. Will this decision save/improve our finances? Do our own personal decisions, or decisions in which we are involved, reach beyond the parameter of financial gain for me, my company, my organisation?

Matthew 20:1–16

' "Have I no right to do what I like with my own? Why
be envious because I am generous."
Thus the last will be first, and the first last.' (20:15–16)

These words come at the end of the parable of the labourers, in
which the last-hour labourers have been paid the same wage as
those who have worked all day. It is another example of the
difference between God's thinking and our own.

God, as described by Jesus in the parables, is imprudent in
financial matters and disastrous in industrial relations! We need
to ponder our uneasiness with this or any other parable, for our
uneasiness can become a door to a new understanding of God
and of ourselves.

If we think of God as an employer, like one of us, then his
action in paying the last-minute labourers the same as those
who have worked all day is certainly unfair. In response to the
question, 'Why did God create?', the great medieval
theologian, Thomas Aquinas, answered, 'Because Goodness,
of its nature, overflows!' Goodness is not calculating, but
rejoices in giving, both to the deserving and to the un-
deserving. Perhaps we can catch a glimpse of this in our
reactions to some wonderful event. As a child, I can remember
the scramble after a wedding, when the bride and groom threw
money out of the car window as they drove away. Their own
happiness had to be expressed in giving. They did not throw

with care, ensuring that those who had been waiting longest received most.

There is great comfort for most of us in the parable of the labourers. God's giving is utterly free, utterly gratuitous. It does not depend on our past performance, our achievements, or our virtuous record: the first shall be last and the last first. Therefore it is a waste of time to spend our time and energy in regretting the past, in nurturing our sense of guilt. We have to acknowledge our past and recognise our guilt, for unless we do so, we cannot know the goodness of God, who forgives us, accepts us, welcomes us, and who re-creates out of our destructiveness. What is important for us is the present. God is gracious to us in every moment of our lives. From a human point of view our lives may seem to have been a failure, but God's thinking is much broader and deeper than our own. Our present attitude of mind is much more important than our past failures, and God's goodness is more important than our sinfulness.

PRAYER
God, transform my heart, shrivelled by careful calculation, and fill it with your spirit of reckless generosity.

EXERCISE
Reflect on the moments you have enjoyed today. Were they rewards for your hard work, or did they just come unexpectedly?

Matthew 22:1–10

> So these servants went out on to the roads and collected
> together everyone they could find, bad and good alike,
> and the wedding hall was filled with guests. (22:10)

In this parable Jesus describes God as a king, who provides a
banquet for his son's wedding. The invited guests, too preoccupied
with their own interests, reject the invitation, so the King sends
out his servants to 'go to the crossroads in the town and invite
everyone you can find to the wedding'.

In the parable, God is pictured as a God of lavish generosity,
but touchy if those invited do not accept his hospitality! The
parable reflects Jesus's rejection by his own people. It also reflects
the nature of God's Kingdom, that it is open to all people of all
nations, races and classes, whether they be virtuous or not.

It is good to notice our own felt reactions when we read this.
Does the news that God's Kingdom is open to all delight or
distress us? If it distresses us, why? Perhaps we would prefer a
more selective Kingdom, including, of course, ourselves. We are
touching on the differences between God's thinking and our own.
We prefer an exclusive Kingdom for us and those like us; God
welcomes everyone, including the people we can't stand. It has
been said that 'We are as near to God as we are to the person we
like least.'

When we are surprised and delighted by some good news, it is
amazing how quickly we can forget grudges, anxieties and hurts

which had been plaguing us, and we can suddenly become genuinely well-disposed to those we formerly disliked. In such a situation we are touching on 'that which is of God' within us.

If we are going to be happy rather than miserable at the heavenly banquet, we may as well start now to become more aware of our own mental conditioning, which divides the world into 'them', the vast majority, and 'us', a tiny fraction, or even 'me', tinier still, and ask God to teach us how to be more welcoming to all. We are dependent on each other in ways we have hardly begun to understand. Rejection of the other is a rejection of God, and also of ourselves.

PRAYER
God, let our hearts know such joy in your presence that the thought of anyone being excluded from it would cause us great sadness.

EXERCISE
Reflect on the phrase, 'God welcomes all, wicked and good alike', and talk to God about it.

Matthew 18:23–35

'I cancelled all that debt of yours when you appealed to
me. Were you not bound, then, to have pity on your
fellow servant just as I had pity on you?' (18:32–3)

The God of the Covenant is a God lavish in giving, financially
imprudent, and who abhors stinginess. In this parable God is
presented as a king who waives the debts of a man who owes him
ten-thousand talents, the equivalent of several million pounds.
However, when that same man throws into prison a debtor who
owes him about five pounds, the king sends for him. ' "I cancelled
all that debt of yours when you appealed to me. Were you not
bound, then, to have pity on your fellow servant just as I had pity
on you?" And in his anger the master handed him over to the
torturers till he should pay all his debt.'

We need to pray to live in the consciousness of God's goodness
to us. If we could know it, we would want to show that same
generosity to others. It is because we do not know God's goodness
to us that we can become complacent about ourselves and more
judgmental and condemnatory of others. If we could really know
ourselves we would realise that, just as there is no height of
heroism or virtue which is beyond our capabilities, so also there
is no depth of depravity or wickedness of which we are not
capable. If we have not reached those depths, we would know
that this is not due to any merit on our part. We would be unable
to join in the choruses of disapproval and condemnation in which

we love to indulge when some scandal is uncovered.

The nineteenth-century Russian Orthodox mystic, Seraphim of Sarov, wrote, 'Always be gentle and never condemn another, even if you catch them in an evil act.' The reason he gives is that we could never condemn another if we really appreciated the goodness of God to ourselves.

If we are to know something of the depths of God's generosity to us, we have to acknowledge our own individual and corporate wrongdoing. The most destructive element in sinfulness is its blinding effect. We can feel pleased with ourselves and self-righteous, while doing immense damage to others. An example of blinding corporate wrongdoing is the crushing burden of debt which rich countries are imposing on the poor, subjecting whole nations to economic slavery, causing millions to die of starvation, depriving the nations of the money required for health care, housing, education and development. We pride ourselves on our sense of justice and fair play. When individual citizens in our own country fall into bankruptcy we have laws which protect them and their families from starvation. But when we commit injustice on a national scale, bringing death to other nations, we can remain undisturbed.

PRAYER
God, open our eyes, shatter our complacency, flood us with your spirit of generosity, so that we may have the strength and courage to campaign for the lifting of the death-dealing national debt on poor countries.

EXERCISE
'When evil is done on a national scale, co-operation and collusion is considered patriotic.' Reflect on this statement and on Jesus's words: 'Men will seize you and persecute you; they will hand you over to the synagogues and to imprisonment, and bring you before kings and governors because of my name.'

Matthew 18:21–22

Then Peter went up to him and said, 'Lord, how often must I forgive my brother if he wrongs me? As often as seven times?'

Jesus answered, 'Not seven, I tell you, but seventy-seven times.'

In all the Old Testament passages in which God threatens his people with terrible punishments, there is always a note of mercy, 'Though your sins are like scarlet, they shall be as white as snow' (Isaiah 1:18). The God of the Covenant is a forgiving God.

The test of our faith in God is our ability to forgive. When we try to forgive, we become more aware of the shallowness and fragility of our faith. The offence done to us can infect our whole being, becoming the focal point of all our thoughts and feelings. It is as though the offence possesses us, joining forces with all the other offences done to us, whether real or imagined, until our whole being is crying out for vengeance. We may occasionally succeed in praying to be able to forgive, but the feelings of hurt and resentment soon regroup and sweep away our act of forgiveness.

We can assure ourselves that there is no need to forgive until the offender asks for pardon. As long as they fail to do so, we feel less bad about our own vengeful feelings. This is a deception. In our hearts we must be ready to forgive. Insofar as we can, we must pray for and do good to the offender, even if the offender does not ask for forgiveness.

Our offenders can become, unwittingly, our greatest benefactors, for they make us aware of our inability to forgive, or to do anything virtuous. They therefore force us to ask God to take over and to forgive through us. So the first benefit of the offender is to set us on the path of spiritual poverty. The other benefit is that we come to understand more clearly the meaning of Jesus's advice to Peter, that he must forgive seventy-seven times. This advice used to seem to me not only excessive but singularly ineffective. If I forgive, and my brother continues to offend another seventy-six times, then my forgiveness does not seem to be helping him! But in trying to forgive, we become more aware of the many-layered nature of our consciousness. Having forgiven once, we find further layers of consciousness within us which have not yet forgiven; not just seven layers, but seventy-seven, and as we reach deeper layers, we have to learn to forgive the one offence again and again. So our offender has helped us to understand the nature of faith and of Jesus's teaching.

PRAYER
God, bless, protect and guide all those who have ever offended me, whether in reality, or in my imagination, and help me to work for their good as though it were my own.

EXERCISE
If you are finding forgiveness difficult, then, in imagination, sit down with your enemy and with Jesus. Tell your enemy how hurt you are, then pause and allow the enemy to speak. Then let Jesus speak to you both.

Matthew 20:20–28

'For the Son of Man himself did not come to be served
but to serve, and to give his life as a ransom for many.'

(20:28)

Mother Zebedee has asked Jesus that her two sons, James and
John, should have the top places in the Kingdom. Jesus challenges
the two sons, 'Can you drink the cup that I am going to drink?'
(He has just been telling them of his coming Passion and death.)
They assure him that they can. He accepts their offer, but adds
that it is not for him to award top places in the Kingdom.

Mother Zebedee's request annoys the other disciples, so Jesus
tells them, 'You know that among the pagans the rulers lord it
over them, and their great men make their authority felt. This is
not to happen among you. No, anyone who wants to be great
among you must be your servant, and anyone who wants to be
first among you must be your slave. For the Son of Man did not
come to be served . . .'

In the Gospels, Jesus says very little about the future Church,
but on one point he is very clear, namely on the way in which
authority is to be exercised. The Church is to be 'a light to the
Gentiles', so this understanding of authority has universal
relevance and is not restricted to 'churchy' affairs.

In all human conflict lies a power struggle: an individual,
group or nation insists on imposing its will on those who are
opposed to it, usually justifying the action in high-flown language

about legitimate defence of rights or of freedom. Conflict takes many forms, from world wars between nations to frozen silences between individuals. A first step in any conflict resolution is to persuade the opposing parties to listen to one another. We find it difficult to listen to those opposed to us because we are convinced of the rightness of our cause and the wrongness of the opposition's. The strength of our conviction is proportionate to the narrowness of our mental vision, which cannot see beyond our own personal, or group advantage. Jesus's teaching on the exercise of authority is calling us to a new way of perceiving ourselves. Our true advantage must include the advantage of others, for their good is our good, their loss is, ultimately, our loss.

In this passage, Jesus expresses his deepest desire, which dominates his life, 'for the Son of Man did not come to be served, but to serve, and to give his life as a ransom for many'.

PRAYER

God, you created me in your own image. Help me to discover you in the longing of my heart, to be able to serve, and to give my life that others may live.

EXERCISE

In your own obituary, would you prefer to be remembered as the person who always dominated and controlled every situation, or as the person who had a gift for making other people feel that they mattered and had something important to contribute?

Mark 9:35–50

'Anyone who is not against us is for us.' (9:40)

John has come to Jesus and announced, 'Master, we saw a man who is not one of us casting out devils in your name, and because he is not one of us we tried to stop him.' Jesus replies, 'You must not stop him – anyone who is not against us is for us.' The next verse contains one of the harshest of Jesus's sayings, 'If your hand should cause you to sin, cut it off; it is better for you to enter into life crippled than to have two hands and go to hell. And if your foot should cause you to sin, cut it off. And if your eye should cause you to sin, tear it out.' If this passage were followed to the letter, then we would all be cripples, so what does it mean?

In the light of the rest of Jesus's teaching and from the parable of the wedding feast, it is obvious that one meaning is that the Kingdom of God is all-inclusive: the Covenant is with all peoples and with all creation.

The second meaning is that in order to preserve this divine inclusivity, then those who try to turn the Kingdom into a kind of exclusive club are to be themselves excluded, no matter how important and significant they may be for the Body of the Church; even if they be the hand, the foot, or the eye. The Church must be inclusive.

What an astonishing message for our churches, which can only remain divided because they are exclusive, yet justify their exclusivity in the name of Christ, who warned them so severely against such conduct!

Working for the visible unity of all Christian churches is not an optional extra for 'chummy' Christians. Christian unity belongs to the very heart of the Gospel. Unity does not mean uniformity, nor does it mean that we should pretend that our differences do not exist. Working for unity means that we should concentrate our attention on that which unites us, rather than on that which divides, and we should co-operate with each other insofar as we can. If we all worked together for the good of our community, whatever its religious allegiance or lack of it, we would grow in unity because God is the God of compassion. And if we pray together, then the Spirit of Christ will draw us together. This is happening in many places, but we still have a long way to go.

Because the Covenant is universal, our work for unity cannot be limited to working among Christians of other denominations, but must include inter-faith work, and work with those who profess to have no faith.

PRAYER

God, you hold all things and all people in unity. Enlighten our minds and hearts so that we may recognise this unity and respect the wonderful variety of your creation.

EXERCISE

Read the Acts of the Apostles, the story of the early Church, in light of this teaching of Jesus. Then reflect on your own experience of Church today.

Matthew 25:31–46

'For I was hungry and you never gave me food.' (25:42)

If a religious leader is asked, 'What is the most important thing we can do in life?', we should expect that leader to say something about God, prayer, religious observance and belief. If Jesus had never given this description of the Final Judgment in his own lifetime, but was to reappear in modern Britain and deliver it in a broadcast to the nation, there would be uproar in many sections of the Christian churches. 'The man is a humanist'; 'He has reduced the God of mystery to being a do-gooder'; 'He has no sense of divine transcendence'; 'If he is allowed to go on like this, he will empty the churches in no time'; 'He sounds like an old-fashioned socialist.'

Where are we to find God and how are we to serve him? In the Torah, the Jewish Law, which draws out the implications of God's Covenant, two-thirds of the Law is concerned with relations with other people, not just other Jews, but also with the stranger. Jesus makes this teaching even more explicit: we are to find God in our relationships with one another; as we serve one another, so we are serving God. We may wish God had not ordained things in this way, but our wishes cannot change the truth of things.

We keep trying to escape this truth. 'Poverty is a punishment from God for sinfulness' – the implication being that it is therefore against the will of God to try to alleviate it. Or, 'People have only their own fecklessness to blame for their poverty.'

We are made in the image of God. God's life is a life of complete sharing between the three Divine Persons, so that the Father has nothing which is not equally possessed by the Son and the Holy Spirit. Jesus said, 'Unless you lose your life, you cannot find it.'

Today, there is great emphasis on self-development among many of those who are relatively secure. We can only realise our full potential when we lose ourselves, that is, when we stop worrying about our personal development, and pay more attention to the needs of those around, as though they were ourselves. Persons are relations, not isolated units. When our focus is on answering the needs of others, then our lives are God-centred, whether or not we are conscious of this. After the Second World War, the writer and atheistic humanist, Albert Camus, gave a talk to some French priests, urging them to be true to Jesus's Sermon on the Mount, and to join with himself and other humanists in working for the promotion of justice and peace throughout the world. If Jesus had been present, I am sure he would have said to Camus at the end of it, 'You are not far from the Kingdom of God.'!

PRAYER
God, rid our minds of all those false images of you which allow us to see you as distinct from those who are hungry, homeless, sick and imprisoned.

EXERCISE
What do you consider to be of ultimate importance in life? How much time, energy and attention do you give to it.

Matthew 23:1–36

'Alas for you, scribes and Pharisees, you hypocrites.'
(23:13)

In the opening verse of this chapter, Jesus asserts the legitimate authority of the scribes and Pharisees: 'The scribes and Pharisees occupy the chair of Moses. You must therefore do what they tell you and listen to what they say.' Then follows a vitriolic attack on these same authorities – the passage peppered with 'hypocrites', 'blind guides', 'whited sepulchres' and 'serpents'.

Why this rage? Because the scribes and Pharisees are using God, the God of compassion, to tyrannise for their own advantage. 'They tie up heavy burdens and lay them on people's shoulders, but will they lift a finger to help them? Not they!' Jesus's anger, like Yahweh's, delivered through the Old Testament prophets, is the obverse of his love for God and for God's people.

Why do the evangelists include these passages in their Gospels? Presumably because they recognised those same pharisaic tendencies among those in authority in the early Church.

Robust criticism of those in authority in the Church and in the state can be a virtue, rather than a vice or a sign of disloyalty; yet those in authority can so emphasise the virtues of obedience, loyalty and fidelity that any critic of authority in the Church can be labelled as unorthodox, or lacking in faith, which silences the timid. The danger then is that conformity to Church rules and regulations can become a substitute for obedience to the Spirit of

God; idolatry to a system replacing worship of the living God, the very attitude which Jesus condemns in this chapter.

The Spirit of God is a Spirit of truth and of freedom. The entire justification of ecclesiastical structure and organisation lies in the fact that it enables us to achieve greater freedom in listening and responding to the Spirit of God at work in all things and in all people. And the Church's role in society is to speak the truth in love, while questioning and criticising without fear or favour, whenever authority exercises power to its own advantage and to the detriment of its subjects. It is generally a good sign when the Church is criticised by state authorities, and a bad sign when it is assumed to be their ally.

PRAYER
God, teach us to respect and listen to those in authority in the Church, but give us the grace to listen above all to your teaching in our hearts.

EXERCISE
Compose your own attack on the scribes and Pharisees of today, who may not be religious people, but those who adopt a high moral tone in order to subdue others and impose their own will. Then ask if your anger is coming from love? If so, what action are you going to take?

Luke 22:14–38

'This is my body which will be given for you; do this as
a memorial of me.' (22:19)

In Duntocher, on the outskirts of Glasgow, ecumenical relations
among the children were so advanced that their games included
running in and out of the Catholic church. One little Protestant
boy was so taken with this church that he began attending Mass
on Sundays with his Catholic friends. One Sunday, he joined them
when they went up to receive Holy Communion. On returning to
his place he received a sharp dig in the ribs from his Catholic
friend who whispered, 'If you swallow that, we'll bash you.'!

One of the tragedies of our Christian disunity is that we are
unable to celebrate the Eucharist together. The Roman Catholic
Eucharist is for Roman Catholics only; the Orthodox Eucharist
for Orthodox only, and there are innumerable books and articles
justifying these restrictions.

In these readings we have been looking at aspects of God's
Covenant with the whole of creation. For Christians, Jesus is the
image of the unseen God, revealer of the full meaning of this
Covenant.

At the Last Supper, Jesus took a piece of bread, blessed it and
broke it, saying 'This is me, given for you.' This is a sign,
signifying a reality, the reality of God, who is continuously giving
himself at all times and in all places and to all peoples. The
theologians of the early Church spoke of the whole of creation as

a sacrament, a sign and an effective sign of God's presence. Every bush is burning, if only we had the eyes to see.

'Do this in my memory.' This means far more than celebrating formal eucharistic liturgies. It is an invitation to become Eucharist, to allow the self-giving of God to be expressed in all our thinking and acting, in all our relationships, as individuals, as Church and as nation. This is to be the characteristic of the people of the Covenant, as it was the characteristic of Jesus's life. 'I have come that you may have life, and have it more abundantly.'

In his autobiography, the religious broadcaster, Gerald Priestland, describes having tea with the Archbishop of Canterbury. The Archbishop asked him if he did not, as a Quaker, feel deprived of the Eucharist. Gerald Priestland replied that, as a Quaker, he believed that every meal was a Eucharist. 'Whereupon,' he said, 'the Archbishop looked at his petit-four with greater respect.'!

PRAYER
God, we thank you for the gift of life, for the mystery of your creation, but above all we thank you for the gift of yourself in the Eucharist, pledge of our resurrection and of our unity with you and with all creation, and we pray that we may know its loving power in our lives, now and always.

EXERCISE
If you were to understand the Eucharist in this way and live it in practice, what difference would it make in your own life and in the life of the nation?

John 13:1–20

'Jesus knew that the Father had put everything into his
hands . . . he then poured water into a basin and began to
wash his disciples' feet . . . If I, then, the Lord and
Master have washed your feet, you should wash each
other's feet.' (13:3–5, 14)

The remaining Scripture texts are from the accounts of Jesus's
Passion, death and Resurrection. In Christian understanding,
these events are the sealing of God's Covenant with us. 'God
became a human being so that human beings might become God,'
as the second-century St Ireneus wrote. In Jesus, God has become
one of us, has entered into our weakness, our sinfulness and our
death. He is risen again, and we shall rise with him.

Jesus's Passion and death took place two-thousand years ago,
but the Spirit, who lived in Jesus and raised him from the dead,
now lives in us, continuing God's work of liberation. There is no
depth of human experience, no suffering, no tragedy, no
sinfulness in which God is not present, hovering over the chaos,
bringing life out of death, good out of evil. When we look at the
injustices of our world, the brutalities of ethnic cleansing, the
torture of the innocent, the blight of the arms trade with its
massive cost in innocent lives, at the plight of almost a billion
people, starving and destitute because of the greed of others,
whose lifestyle, and the atmospheric pollution it causes, threatens
all human life on earth, we can sink into despair, which is why

we prefer not to think about these problems.

What can we do? Despair has been described as 'the last refuge of the ego'. Our despair arises out of the atheist part of ourselves, the part which discounts God and thinks that everything depends on me and my power. In contemplating Jesus's Passion and death we must let our despair enter into our prayer, so that faith in God can reach our hidden depths of atheism.

In praying the Passion, just be present in the scene as though it were happening now. Watch and gaze. The Jesus you contemplate is closer to you than you are to yourself, and he will teach you.

Jesus knew that all power had been given to him by his Father. Instead of imprisoning all those who were opposed to him and his message, he girded himself with a towel and began to wash the feet of his disciples, including Judas, who was about to betray him.

What revolutionary teaching! Power is to be exercised in loving service of one another. The God of the Covenant is a God who serves, who washes feet, who gives bread to the hungry, drink to the thirsty, and shelter to the homeless poor. To live in God is to let God be this kind of God to us and through us. So Jesus says, 'You must wash each other's feet.'

PRAYER
God, help us so to enter into the mystery of your Passion and death that we can know the power of your love at work in our powerlessness.

EXERCISE
Imagine Jesus washing your feet, then speak with him.

John 13:21–14:1

'Do not let your hearts be troubled. Trust in God still,
and trust in me.' (14:1)

These words of Jesus come immediately after he has told Peter,
'I tell you most solemnly, before the cock crows you will have
disowned me three times.'

We cannot know what Peter felt when he heard this pre-
diction of his betrayal, but we can conjecture. Jesus had said,
'Where I am going, you cannot follow me now: you will follow
me later.' Peter replies, 'Why can I not follow you now? I will
lay down my life for you.' Peter is being utterly sincere. To be
told that he will disown Jesus three times before cockcrow
must have been devastating. It is as though Jesus says, 'Lay
down your life for me? You haven't got a life to lay down. You
utter fine statements, but there is no core to your being. You
are a non-person.'

Then Jesus says, 'Do not let your heart be troubled.'! He gives
the reason, 'Trust in God still, and trust in me.' These two brief
sentences give us the essential instructions we need for our
spiritual journey.

Hear these words of Jesus being said to you now and let them
hover over your own anxieties and troubles. It may be anxiety
about your own inadequacy, your own failings, or about your
own sense of helplessness in the face of the evils around you.
Contemplation can give us an inner knowledge which no amount

of Bible study can ever provide; the kind of knowledge of which the prophet Isaiah speaks:

> When the Lord has given you the bread of suffering and the water of distress, he who is your teacher will hide no longer, and you will see your teacher with your own eyes . . . Your ears will hear these words behind you, 'This is the way, follow it.'
>
> (Isaiah 30:20–1)

And the way is the way of complete trust. In Jesus, God is telling us to change our perception, to stop regarding ourselves as islands called 'Me'. We live in God. Our ultimate identity is not in our notion of ourselves, but in God, always greater, always faithful, whose goodness is greater than our sinfulness, whose love is stronger than our betrayals, whose truth is greater than our denials.

PRAYER
God, give me the courage to face my own fears and anxieties, so that in facing them I may know you, my only rock, refuge and strength.

EXERCISE
Have you ever experienced desperation? Recall the experience, look at the assumptions underlying the experience, then hand over your desperation to God.

Mark 14:32–52

'My soul is sorrowful to the point of death. Wait here, and keep awake.' (14:35)

God's Covenant with us is cosmic. When we think of this in spatial terms, it means little to us, for it is too great for our minds to grasp; it is a truth outside of us. But God's Covenant is with the microcosm as well as the macrocosm; it includes our inner world of mind and heart, the depths of our being. In Jesus, God enters our inner world of consciousness.

'My soul is sorrowful to the point of death.' God's Covenant reaches into the depths of our sadness, despair and guilt. In St Paul's words, 'He became sin for us . . . that we might become the goodness of God' (2 Corinthians 5:21). There is no depth of human suffering, no agony of mind we can experience, where God, the divine alchemist, is not present, transforming the base metal of our inner experience into something of infinite value, not just for us, but for the benefit of all creation.

'Wait here, and keep awake.' In our own sadness, disappointment and despair, we can focus our attention on God, present within it. In the light of this truth we can begin to see the sources of our pain, distinguishing the pain which arises within us from the destruction of our own kingdom of status, reputation and personal ambition, from the pain which arises from our empathy with other people's pain, the pain of the world.

There is an ancient Jewish tradition that the world is upheld in each generation by thirty-six Just Men, the *Lamed-waf*, into whom all the griefs of the world are poured. Even if one of them were lacking, the sufferings of humankind would poison even the souls of the newborn, and humanity would stifle with a single cry. The Lamed-waf are the 'absorbers' of the world's grief; its saviours, although they may live unconscious of their universal role. As Christians, we believe that Jesus has taken on this role of a Lamed-waf, living and dying for the sins of the world. If we, in our suffering, can wait and keep awake, calling on him in our pain, then our pain will become redemptive, not only for ourselves, but also for the world, even though the source of our pain may be our own bruised ego. In his Passion, it is as though all the sinfulness of the world is concentrated into one great mass and hurled at Jesus, who absorbs it in his person transforming it into something life-giving. Christian tradition sees this truth symbolised in the piercing of Jesus's side by the lance, whence comes the blood and water in which we are redeemed.

PRAYER

Lord, may all that is within you flow into me, so that my life bears witness to your goodness.

EXERCISE

Offer whatever pain and inner darkness you experience to God and pray 'Take it, and transform it into a blessing for me and for others.'

John 18:28–19:16

'Mine is not a kingdom of this world.' (18:36)

These words are spoken by Jesus in answer to Pilate's question, 'Are you the King of the Jews?', and it reveals the great gulf between God's ways and our ways.

Pilate is in a difficult position. He is the representative of Roman law and order in Palestine, one of the most troublesome outposts of the Empire. The Jewish authorities have handed Jesus over as a criminal, a blasphemer and a threat to Caesar. Pilate tries to be fair, so as a first step he makes use of his privilege of offering freedom to one criminal at the time of the Passover. He offers the Jews the choice of Barabbas, a condemned brigand, or Jesus. The crowds choose Barabbas and demand Jesus's death. By giving in to their request Pilate will placate the Jews, keep the peace and so please Caesar. By refusing their request he could be held responsible for a Jewish uprising, and for having failed to act on a warning given by the Jewish authorities themselves. Pilate had already been in trouble with Rome for his conduct as governor of Judea, so he had to be careful. He ordered that Jesus be kept in custody and scourged, placating the Jewish authorities for the time being. His action was prudent in the world's eyes. Prisons throughout the world contain men and women who are considered a threat to national security, although they have committed no criminal offence.

Jesus explains the meaning of his kingship to Pilate. 'Yes, I am a king. I was born for this, I came into the world for this: to bear witness to the truth.' 'Truth?' said Pilate, 'What is that?' The Kingdom of God is a kingdom of truth. There is a short story by Saki (H.H. Munro) about a cat called Tobermory, which has learned to talk but speaks only the truth, causing havoc at a house-party of very respectable people. The story is a parable. Truth is devastating for any individual, group or nation which finds its security in lies. 'The truth will set you free', but we may have to go through hell on the way. The God of truth has called us into a Covenant. 'Be truthful, as I the Lord your God am truthful.' If we can be truthful before God, we become aware that we are naked, defenceless and without any self-justification. We can only cry, 'Lord, have mercy on me a sinner.' But with that cry, as with the tax-collector in the parable, we return to a right relationship with God.

PRAYER
God, lead us out of the prison of our self-deceit so that our eyes may be opened and we may recognise you at work in every detail of our lives.

EXERCISE
Reflect on Jeremiah's words: 'The heart is more devious than any other thing; perverse, too: who can pierce its secrets?'

John 19:17–37

'One of the soldiers pierced his side with a lance: and immediately there came out blood and water.' (19:34)

During the Easter Vigil service in the Roman Catholic tradition the 'Exsultet', a song of praise to the risen Christ, calls on the whole of creation to join in praise and thanksgiving. The song includes the extraordinary phrase, 'O happy sin of Adam, which merited such a Redeemer.'

The first sentence of the Bible introduces this theme: 'There was darkness over the deep, and God's spirit hovered over the water.' God creates order and life out of chaos, even out of the destruction caused by sin. When Joseph, who has risen to become Pharaoh's steward, meets his brothers, who had originally sold him to passing traders, he tells them, 'You thought to do me evil, but God has turned it all to good account.' When human beings had done their worst to Jesus, image of the unseen God, and pierced his side with a lance, God's answer is the blood and water which, for St John, is the source of new life for all humankind, the Covenant sealed in God's own blood.

We speak of God as the God of mystery, the God who is always 'other', the God who is always greater. As human beings we can have an inkling of what love is. To contemplate the pierced Jesus is to catch a glimpse of the immanence of the God who is transcendent, a God whose love and whose goodness go beyond our thinking and our imagining.

At the beginning of his book of *Spiritual Exercises*, Ignatius Loyola advises those who give these Exercises to others to be as brief as possible in offering Scripture passages for prayer. 'It is not quantity of knowledge which fills and satisfies the soul, but the inner understanding and relish of the truth.' We have only to gaze at the figure on the cross, his side pierced with a lance. This is the nature of the God holding me in being as I gaze; the God holding all things in being.

It may help you in your gazing to keep saying to yourself, 'He does this for me.' Don't try to think things out, just gaze. The heart has a language which is beyond words. If you practise praying in this way, you may have no great thoughts at the end of your prayer, but your perception of things begins to change and the world becomes 'charged with the grandeur of God'.

PRAYER
God, still my mind and heart, and give me the grace to wonder at the limitlessness of your love.

EXERCISE
Just gaze at the pierced Jesus. Don't try to think or theorise, but let your heart respond.

John 20:19–21

In the evening of that same day, the first day of the week,
the doors were closed in the room where the disciples
were, for fear of the Jews. Jesus came and stood among
them. 'Peace be with you,' he said, and showed them his
hands and his side. (20:19)

Belief in the Resurrection is not simply belief in an event which
occurred two-thousand years ago; it is belief in a present reality:
Jesus who lived and died is now risen and is Lord of all creation.
And the Spirit who lived in Jesus and raised him from the dead
now lives in us.

Although the Gospel accounts of the Resurrection are very
different, there is a common pattern. The people to whom the
risen Jesus appears are usually in a negative mood. In the Gospel
of Mark, the women are terrified; Mary Magdalene is distraught,
the disciples in the Upper Room are afraid, and the two disciples
on the road to Emmaus are disconsolate. When Christ does appear
to them they are usually slow to recognise him. Once they have
recognised him, they are commissioned to go and tell the news to
the others.

The experience of many of us today still follows the same
pattern. It is often after we have experienced some kind of death,
a family bereavement, or failure, or threat to our health, that
Christ's Resurrection takes on new meaning for us. Realising that
he is risen from the dead, that his Spirit is within and around us,

permeating all peoples and all things is a knowledge which only slowly seeps through our consciousness. Although we know our knowledge of his Resurrection will always be incomplete this side of death, it is a life-giving knowledge which we want to share and celebrate with others. The book of the Acts of the Apostles continues the Gospels' Resurrection accounts, showing the early Church growing through the power of the risen Christ and spreading among the pagans.

The God of the Cosmic Covenant is the God of each one of us. Imagine the scene in the Upper Room as though it were happening now, and hear the risen Lord calling you by your name and saying to you, 'Shalom', and showing you his wounded hands and side. 'Shalom' has a much richer and wider meaning than our word 'peace'. We tend to think of peace as the absence of conflict. 'Shalom' means, 'May you be in a right relationship with God, with yourself, with your neighbour. May you enjoy good health and prosper. May you find peace in conflict and meet death with peace.'

Be still, and let your heart recognise the risen Christ, closer to you than you are to yourself.

PRAYER

Lord, whenever I am locked up in my own fears and worries, let me see you showing me your hands and your side, and hear you saying, 'Shalom! I am always with you and will never leave you.'

EXERCISE

In John's account, it is when he shows his wounded hands and side that Jesus says 'Peace to you'. Reflect on the connection between knowing the peace of Christ and being willing to be vulnerable.

John 21:1–23

After this Jesus said, 'Follow me.' (21:19)

The last chapter of St John's Gospel describes Jesus on the shore of Lake Tiberias. Some of the disciples, including Peter, had gone fishing but failed to catch anything. A stranger on the shore calls out, 'Throw the net to starboard.' They do so and their nets are filled. They then recognise Jesus, who cooks breakfast for them. After breakfast, Jesus puts three questions to Peter.

Greek, in which St John's Gospel was originally written, has many different words for our word 'love'. 'Philia', for example, means a love which contains an element of self-interest – 'I love you because we are so alike and share the same interests', or 'I love you because you make me feel alive.' Philia is the love on which friendship is based. 'Agape', the purest form of love, indicates a totally selfless love, 'I love you because you are you, and not for any benefit you may be to me.'

Jesus first asks, 'Peter do you love me more than these others do?', using the Greek verb 'Agapeis', as though to ask, 'Peter, do you love me with a totally selfless love?' Peter answers, 'Yes, Lord, you know I love you', but Peter uses the word 'Phileo', meaning, 'I love you, but with a bit of self-interest.' Jesus says, 'Feed my lambs.' In his second question to Peter, Jesus asks ' "Agapas" me?', and Peter again answers, 'Yes, Lord, you know I "phileo" you.' Jesus says, 'Look after my sheep.' The third time Jesus asks, ' "Phileis" me?', as though to ask, 'Do you love me

111

even as a friend loves a friend, partly from self-interest?' That is why Peter is upset, and answers again, 'Lord, you know everything; you know I love (phileo) you', and Jesus says, 'Feed my sheep.' He tells Peter that when he grows old another will lead him where he would rather not go, and then says, 'Follow me.'

Peter acknowledges that his love for Jesus is contaminated with self-interest. Jesus knows this, but still entrusts him with his mission, 'Feed my sheep.'

God knows our hearts and our fickleness better than we do. He does not choose us because we are strong and virtuous; he chooses the weak and makes them strong. In praying this passage, let your focus be on Jesus calling to you, 'Follow me', rather than on your own inability to follow.

PRAYER

> Be Thou my vision, Lord of my heart.
> Naught be all else to me save that Thou art.
> Thou my best thought in the day and the night
> Waking, or sleeping, my vision Thou art.

EXERCISE

Hear Jesus ask you these same questions. Acknowledge your own inability to love with agape, then hear Jesus say to you, 'Follow me.'

Luke 24:13–35

'And their eyes were opened and they recognised him.'
(24:31)

Luke describes a resurrection appearance of Jesus to two disconsolate disciples on their way from Jerusalem to Emmaus. He appears as a stranger who joins them on the road and asks why they are so downcast. When they explain, the stranger gives them a bit of Bible study. 'Starting with Moses and going through all the prophets, he explained to them the passages throughout the Scriptures that were about himself' (v. 27). On reaching Emmaus, the disciples press the stranger to stay with them. 'Now while he was with them at table, he took bread and said the blessing; then he broke it and handed it to them, and their eyes were opened and they recognised him, but he had vanished from their sight' (vv. 30–2).

They recognised him in the breaking of bread, and once they had recognised him, 'They said to each other, "Did not our hearts burn within us as he talked to us on the road, and explained the Scriptures to us?" ' (v. 32).

'Where is the risen Lord?' In the Gospel accounts, he appears as the stranger on the shore, the stranger on the road, as the gardener when Mary Magdalene visits the empty tomb. As the poet, Gerard Manley Hopkins, expresses it:

Christ, for Christ plays in ten thousand places,

GOD OF COMPASSION

Lovely in limbs, and lovely in eyes not his
To the Father through the features of men's faces.

Eucharist is everywhere, if we have the eyes to recognise it, for
the Church's celebration of the sacrament of the Eucharist is
signifying a reality, namely the self-giving love of God, the heart
of the universe.

> I see his blood upon the rose
> And in the stars the glory of his eyes
> His body gleams amid eternal snows,
> His tears fall from the skies.
>
> (Joseph Plunkett)

And to live true to the Covenant is to allow this self-giving love
of God to flow into us and out from us.

PRAYER
Lord, may the Eucharist we receive take possession of our lives,
so that in all our encounters, we pass on something of your self-
giving to those we meet.

EXERCISE
Recall moments of your life when you have recognised him in
the breaking of bread or in the sharing of another's joy or sorrow.

Acts 2:1–13

'They were all filled with the Holy Spirit, and began to speak foreign languages as the Spirit gave them the gift of speech.' (2:4)

'Christ is risen', but where is he to be found? The Gospels describe Resurrection appearances to certain men and women who were his disciples: the Acts of the Apostles continues the story of Christ's Resurrection, his risen life now manifest in the lives of his followers. The pattern of his life and death continues, for the disciples preach, heal and suffer persecution. Stephen is stoned to death; like Jesus he dies praying for his enemies.

Acts 2:1–13 describes the coming of the Holy Spirit to the disciples on the day of Pentecost. People are gathered in Jerusalem from many different nations, yet they all understand the disciples in their own language – intimation of the universality of the Spirit.

The first major crisis of the early Church concerned the demands which must be made of pagan converts, whether or not they must obey all the precepts of Jewish law. The apostles held a council at Jerusalem, and their conclusion was: 'It has been decided by the Holy Spirit and ourselves not to saddle you with any burden beyond these essentials: you are to abstain from food sacrificed to idols, from blood, from the meat of strangled animals and from fornication. Avoid these and you will do what is right' (Acts 15:28).

Christian belief is summed up in the phrase, 'Jesus is Lord.' The Spirit of God is poured out on all creation. The temptation of all Christians is to diminish God and to restrict the Spirit, limiting it to Christians, then limiting it to those Christians only who adhere to particular creeds, rules, regulations and observances. As different Christian groups insist on different regulations, we end up with a very divided Church which is no longer 'a sign to the Gentiles', stifling the Spirit within the Churches themselves.

The phrase, 'It has been decided by the Holy Spirit and ourselves' is fascinating and all-important for all Christians in all their decisions. St Paul wrote, 'The Spirit, which lived in Jesus and raised him from the dead, now lives in you.' This is the heart of the matter. God's Covenant is with all creation. Creation has evolved through billions of years till humankind appeared. Humankind is what God could become, in Jesus, so that human beings could share in the life and love of God, so that our spirit and God's Spirit should become as one. Attentiveness to the Spirit, the Spirit of love and compassion for all creation, is the purpose of all human life.

PRAYER
Come, Holy Spirit, and kindle in us the fire of your love for all peoples, of all nations.

EXERCISE
Reflection: 'Our first task in approaching another people, another culture, another religion, is to take off our shoes, for the place we are approaching is holy. Else we may find ourselves treading on men's dreams. More serious still, we may forget that God was here before our arrival' (Max Warren, Secretary of the Church Missionary Society).

Colossians 1:15–20

'Because God wanted all perfection to be found in him
and all things to be reconciled through him and for him,
everything in heaven and everything on earth, when he
made peace by his death on the cross.' (1:19–20)

God is in everyone and in all things, and God is a God of love, of
compassion, of mercy-filled justice, of reconciliation. All
creation is a sacrament of God, that is, a sign and an effective
sign of God's presence. Everyone and everything is sacred.

These are fine words, but how can we 'earth' them, so that our
lives, as well as our lips can declare this message?

There is a simple exercise which you can do everyday, no
matter how busy you are, and which you can continue after
reading this book. We have already touched on it on page 76,
(Text 29), but here it is described more fully. If we do it once, it
makes very little difference to our lives, but if we do it regularly,
it begins to change the way we perceive reality. The only way in
which we can effect lasting change, whether in ourselves or in
others, is by changing the way we perceive things.

1   Be relaxed and ask God, 'Lord, let my whole being be di-
    rected to your praise and service.'
2   Let the day play back to you in any order. Avoiding any self-
    judgment or moralising, look first at those moments of the
    day you have enjoyed. Relish and thank God for them. They

117

are God's gift to you, signs of God's love.

3   Pray for enlightenment – 'Lord, that I may see'. Now look at your moods and inner feelings during the day, but without judging them. Moods and inner feelings arise from our desires. When our desires are satisfied, we are content; when they are frustrated, we become irritable. We are praying to know the desires and attitudes underlying our moods. Are my desires/attitudes directed to God's Kingdom – am I living to praise, reverence and serve God; or are my desires directed to my personal kingdom – my comfort, wealth, status, honour – wanting creation to praise, reverence and serve me?

4   Express sorrow if you have not been responding to God in the events of the day, knowing God always gives it. Thank God, too, for the times you have responded.

5   Ask God's guidance for tomorrow and entrust yourself to God's goodness, 'like a child in its mother's arms' (Psalms 131:2).

PRAYER

> God, examine me and know my heart,
> test me and know my concerns.
> Make sure that I am not on my way to ruin,
> and guide me on the road of eternity.
> (Psalm 139:23–4)

EXERCISE

Do this exercise daily, now and forever!

Appendix 1

A New Covenant for the Poor

How should the churches mark the 2000th anniversary of the birth of Christ?

All over the world, Christians are starting to prepare for a great religious festival, the 'Jubilee of Jubilees'. We must make sure that no one is excluded from the celebrations.

Pope John Paul II has made the poor of the Third World a special concern in the Catholic Church's preparation for the millennium, even suggesting the goal of the cancellation of third world debt by the year 2000. His apostolic letter, *Tertio Millennio Adveniente*, is a strongly worded message asking us all to help the world's poorest people start the new millennium with a better future: 'In a world like ours, marked by so many conflicts and intolerable social and economic inequalities, a commitment to justice and peace is a necessary precondition for the preparation and celebration of the Jubilee.'

Taking up the Pope's call, many dioceses around the country have signed a *New Covenant with the Poor*, committing them to putting the plight of the world's poor – both at home and abroad – at the heart of their concerns. Parishes and schools in England and Wales are now being invited to make individual Parish Covenants.

A Parish Covenant will be unique to your parish, and reflect local opportunities and circumstances. So that it becomes part of the life of the whole parish, it should be formally adopted during a Sunday Mass or at a special liturgy. Here are some options for how *your* parish can make its own *New Covenant with the Poor*.

The arrival of a new century is a momentous opportunity for bringing about change. So let's use it.

1. Wealth sharing

We promise . . .

- To plan, promote and celebrate the annual CAFOD Harvest and Lent Fast Days
- To participate in CAFOD's *Challenge 2000* scheme and agree to raise _____ per annum
- To respond to emergency appeals in times of disaster
- To give 1 per cent of annual parish income to the poor – half to overseas and half to home
- To plan, promote and celebrate the annual SVP collection
- To support the diocesan welfare society
- To set up a Credit Union
- To encourage an act of fasting and self-denial each Friday of the year
- To use our skills to help others – free legal advice; helping people to read; job searching; language skills; child-minding
- To give our time to visiting the sick, housebound, the elderly, asylum seekers/refugees
- To set aside a percentage of all funds raised for parish buildings or refurbishment projects for the poor at home and overseas

2. Campaigning

We promise . . .

- To actively support CAFOD's Fair Deal for the Poor Campaign and encourage all parishioners (and their families and friends) to sign the CAFOD/Jubilee 2000 debt petition calling for the cancellation of unpayable Third World Debt
- To set up a Traidcraft group and organise a monthly stall after Masses
- To encourage parishioners to buy fairly traded goods and to use fairly traded tea and coffee at parish events
- To support the work of the diocesan/parish Justice & Peace group
- To take part in Church Action on Poverty's millennium initiative, *Pilgrimage Against Poverty*
- To support local ecumenical initiatives aimed at tackling domestic poverty issues such as unemployment and homelessness
- To invite speakers from agencies working with the poor to speak at Mass or give talks to the parish to increase understanding of poverty related issues
- To organise a group to study *The Common Good*, the Bishops' Statement on Catholic Social Teaching
- To lobby the local MP for an increased and effective overseas aid programme

3. Prayer and liturgy

We promise . . .

- To celebrate Mass on the Harvest and Lent Fast Days for the intentions of the hungry of the world
- To include prayers for the poor in the bidding prayers at each Mass

- To include a focus on the needs of the poor in our children's liturgies
- To integrate a justice perspective into our preaching of the Gospel
- To renew our covenant promises each year on the parish feast day
- To encourage the prayer group to regularly pray for the needs of the poor throughout Lent
- To include a justice dimension to the RCIA/catechetical/sacrament preparation programmes
- To use the offertory procession as a focus for our gifts to the poor and an occasion to celebrate what we receive from the poor

These are just a few suggestions to get the discussion in your parish group going. They have a strong CAFOD flavour, but the possibilities are limited only by your own creativity and imagination.

Appendix 2

What follows is a short list of some of the organisations in the churches working in the area of justice, peace and reconciliation:

CAFOD
Romero Close
Stockwell Road
London SW9 9TY
0171-733 7900

The overseas aid and development agency of the Catholic Church, funding development projects throughout the Third World, raising awareness of the causes of poverty and injustice, and campaigning for change.

Catholic Agency for Social Concern (CASC)
39 Eccleston Square
London SW1V 1BX
0171-828 4371

Co-ordinates and develops research for Catholic caring agencies in England and Wales.

Catholic Association for Racial Justice
Unit 2, The Co-op Centre
11 Mowll Street
London SW9 6BG
0171-582 2554

Black and white Christians working together to further racial justice.

Catholic Housing Aid Society (CHAS)
209 Old Marylebone Road
London NW1 5QT
0171-723 7273

CHAS gives advice to people in housing need, develops research and campaigns on housing policy issues.

Catholic Institute for International Relations (CIIR)
Unit 3
Canonbury Yard
190a New North Road
London N1 7BJ
0171-354 0883

A centre for research, analysis and information on issues concerning the developing world; CIIR also recruits qualified and experienced people to work in small-scale development projects overseas.

Christian Aid
P O Box 100
London SE1 7RT
0171-620 4444

An agency of CCBI, funding development projects overseas raising awareness and campaigning against injustice at home.

Christian Ecology Link
Minster Abbey
nr Ramsgate
Kent CT1 4HF
01843-821254

An ecumenical network raising awareness and campaigning on environmental issues.

Christians Abroad
1 Stockwell Green
London SW9 9HP
0171-737 3237

A central channelling agency for people with appropriate skills and qualifications interested in working overseas on a voluntary basis.

Church Action on Poverty
Central Buildings
Oldham Street
Manchester M1 1JT
0161-236 9321

An ecumenical organisation that lobbies and campaigns on poverty issues.

Fellowship of Reconciliation (FOR)
9 Coombe Road
New Malden
Surrey KT3 4QA

An international movement campaigning for peaceful ways of handling conflict.

Jubilee 2000 Coalition
P O Box 100
London SE1 7RT
0171-620 4444

A coalition made up of CAFOD, Christian Aid, Tear Fund and over sixty other agencies and organisations campaigning to cancel the unpayable debts of the world's poorest countries.

National Liaison Committee of Diocesan Justice and Peace Groups
39 Eccleston Square
London SW1V 1BX
0171-834 8550

Co-ordinates the Catholic Church's local network of justice and peace groups.

Pax Christi
9 Henry Road
London N4 2LH
0181-800 4612

Works for a non-violent society in which war will have no place.

Quaker Peace and Service
Friends House
Euston Road
London NW1 2BJ
0171-387 3601

Channels and serves the witness for peace, international service and disarmament.

Scottish Catholic International Aid Fund (SCIAF)
5 Oswald Street
Glasgow G1 4QR
0141-221 4447

SCIAF is the official overseas development agency of the Catholic Church in Scotland. It exists to empower the poor and oppressed and to engage the Scottish public in the process of building a more just world.

Society of St Vincent de Paul
Damascus House
The Ridgeway
London NW7 1EL
0181-906 4119

A worldwide organisation dedicated to alleviating poverty through personal contact and support.

Traidcraft
Kingsway
Gateshead
Tyne and Wear NE11 0NE
0632-873191

Markets handicrafts, tea, coffee and wholefoods from the Third World via mail order and a network of voluntary representatives.

Trocaire
169 Booterstown Avenue
Blackrock
Co. Dublin
(01) 288 5385

The agency for world development of the Irish Catholic Church, helping those in need in developing countries and making Irish people more aware of those needs and our duty in justice towards them.